D0934197

TRANSFORMING POWER OF TECHNOLOGY

TRANSFORMING POWER OF TECHNOLOGY

GUNPOWDER

Richard Worth

CHELSEA HOUSE
PUBLISHERS
A Haights Cross Communications Company

Philadelphia

Frontis: The battle between Samuel de Champlain and his soldiers and the Iroquois Indians at Fort Ticonderoga demonstrated the supremacy of gunpowder over traditional methods of warfare, such as bows and arrows.

CHELSEA HOUSE PUBLISHERS

VP, NEW PRODUCT DEVELOPMENT Sally Cheney
DIRECTOR OF PRODUCTION Kim Shinners
CREATIVE MANAGER Takeshi Takahashi
MANUFACTURING MANAGER Diann Grasse

Staff for GUNPOWDER

EXECUTIVE EDITOR Lee Marcott
ASSOCIATE EDITOR Kate Sullivan
PRODUCTION ASSISTANT Megan Emery
PICTURE RESEARCHER Amy Dunleavy
SERIES AND COVER DESIGNER Keith Trego
LAYOUT 21st Century Publishing and Communications Inc.

A Haights Cross Communications ⌒ Company

http://www.chelseahouse.com

First Printing

1 3 5 7 9 8 6 4 2

Library of Congress Cataloging-in-Publication Data

Worth, Richard.
  Gunpowder / Richard Worth.
    p. cm. -- (Transforming power of technology)
Includes index.
Contents: War begins over gunpowder -- Early methods of warfare -- Gunpowder arrives in Europe -- The conquest of empires -- The first rifles and muskets -- The weapons revolution -- Beyond gunpowder.
  ISBN 0-7910-7448-X
  1. Military art and science--History--Juvenile literature. 2. Gunpowder--History--Juvenile literature. 3. Firepower--History--Juvenile literature. [1. Military art and science--History. 2. Gunpowder--History. 3. Firearms--History. 4. Weapons--History.] I. Title. II. Series.
  U39.W67 2003
  623.4'526--dc21

                                                        2003013634

1

War Begins over Gunpowder

AT ISSUE

Victory in warfare has often depended on a reliable supply of gunpowder. At the start of the American Revolution, both colonial militia and British regulars tried to take control of the same supply of gunpowder, which was stored in Concord, Massachusetts. This led to the first battles of the Revolutionary War on April 19, 1775.

THE REVOLUTIONARY WAR

On a clear, moonlit evening, a small army of British troops left Boston. Led by Major John Pitcairn and Colonel Francis Smith, approximately 700 soldiers were rowed westward across Boston Harbor to the mainland. In the early morning hours of April 19, 1775, they reached the other side. The troops included grenadiers (soldiers armed with grenades) and light infantry, men trained to move quickly to make a surprise attack. Their mission was to advance rapidly westward along the road to Concord, Massachusetts. There, the British believed, American militiamen had stored military supplies, including gunpowder. The colonial army needed the gunpowder to fire their muskets and cannon.

The order to advance against Concord had been given by General Thomas Gage. He was royal governor of Massachusetts and commander in chief of all British forces in North America. Gage was a veteran colonial officer. As a young soldier, he had participated in the French and Indian

War, fought from 1755 to 1763. Gage had led his men in battles from the Ohio Valley to the shores of Lake Champlain in upper New York. After the war, when the French had been driven out of North America, he became governor of Montreal, Canada. In 1774, he was ordered to Boston and was appointed governor of the Massachusetts colony. As governor of the Massachusetts colony, Gage faced a huge task. Relations between the colonists and the British government had become very sour over the last ten years. The French and Indian War had cost Great Britain many millions of dollars and left it with a huge debt. In order to pay off the debt, the British Parliament began to tax the American colonies. Americans protested against being forced to pay these taxes, especially since they had no representatives in Parliament. In 1773, a year before Gage came to Boston, American colonists had protested a tax on tea. Dressed as Mohawk Indians, a group of men boarded British ships in Boston Harbor, seized 342 chests of tea, and dumped them into the water. The incident was called the Boston Tea Party.

In retaliation, the British government closed the port of Boston and Governor Gage was told to stop all trading ships from entering or leaving the port. Since most of the people of Boston depended on trade for their jobs, this was devastating. Massachusetts' colonists vigorously protested this action. They were led by Samuel Adams, who had helped direct the protest against British taxation during the 1760s, and John Hancock, a wealthy colonial merchant. Both men were involved in the Boston Tea Party. They also gathered support from other colonies against the British decision to close the port of Boston.

Tensions in Boston mounted. During the summer, people from the towns surrounding the city had been removing barrels of gunpowder from a nearby storehouse in Charlestown. Governor Gage feared that the colonials might be planning to use the gunpowder to fire their muskets and cannon in a revolt against the British government in Massachusetts. Therefore, in September, he sent more than 200 soldiers to Charlestown. They quickly loaded up 250 half-barrels of gunpowder and placed them under British protection.

It was an entirely peaceful maneuver by Gage and his soldiers. But somehow false reports began to spread that the British had killed several militiamen who had been defending the stores of gunpowder. Suddenly, more than 4,000 colonials grabbed their muskets and began heading from surrounding towns toward Charlestown. Eventually, they discovered that the reports were not true. The men began to return to their homes. But the fact that they had believed the rumors indicated how bad relations had become between the colonials and the British.

Governor Gage was worried that his troops might be attacked in Boston. He decided to build a fortification to defend the long neck that separated the city of Boston from the Massachusetts mainland. The colonials protested that he was trying to prevent any communication between the city and the rest of the colony. Although Gage had tried to close down the Massachusetts Provincial Congress that helped run local affairs in the colony, it continued to meet in Concord. The congress voted to buy military supplies. These included cannon, bullets, muskets, and 1,000 barrels of gunpowder. Late in 1774, the congress also decided to set up regiments of "minutemen." These were soldiers who could turn out "at a minute's notice" to fight against the British.[1] Over the next several months, many towns in Massachusetts established their own regiments of minutemen.

Thus, tensions between the colonials and the British continued to rise. A single incident could easily lead to armed conflict. The first hint that armed conflict was about to begin came in mid-April 1775. Governor Gage began to organize his soldiers for the march toward Concord. Dr. Joseph Warren, one of the leading American patriots in

Boston, discovered that something was about to happen from a "leak" among the British officers. Warren did not know exactly what Governor Gage had planned, but he knew that something would occur on the night of April 18. He decided that something had to be done and met with two other American patriots to discuss the situation — Paul Revere and William Dawes. Revere was a silversmith in Boston and a well-known patriot leader. Dawes was a tanner and a member of the Sons of Liberty, a group of colonials opposed to the British policy of taxation. Dawes and Revere were directed to ride inland and warn the colonial militia that the British were on the march. One of their primary destinations was the town of Lexington, Massachusetts. Hancock and Adams, the men who had organized the Boston Tea Party and other protests against the British, were known to be staying in Lexington. If Gage captured them, it might seriously undermine the colonial resistance.

Revere was rowed across Boston Harbor to the mainland. By 11:00 P.M., he had mounted his horse and was on his way. Riding from town to town, he yelled: "Turn out! Turn out! The Regulars are out!" As historian William Hallahan wrote,

> The designated post rider for each of these towns then stumbled from his bed, saddled his horse, and pounded through the night to a predetermined series of other towns in a network radiating outward from Charlestown, north and westward, waking each town's or village's contingent of . . . Minutemen. And in each village, a new express rider then galloped into the darkness to his preset network of towns—an explosion of riders, all crying the same message! 'Turn out! Turn out! The Regulars are out! The Regulars are out! Pass the word! The Regulars are out!'[2]

Eventually, Revere reached Lexington where he warned

American colonists discovered that British forces were planning to occupy the towns of Lexington and Concord and decided to warn colonial militiamen. On the night of April 18, 1775, Paul Revere rode through towns and villages calling out, "Turn out! Turn out! The Regulars are out!" In each village, a new rider galloped into the darkness to spread the alarm.

Hancock and Adams. Then he rode on toward Concord. Meanwhile, on the green in Lexington, Captain John Parker gathered a small group of 77 militia armed to oppose the British regulars. He told them: "Stand your ground! Don't fire unless fired upon! But if they want to have a war, let it begin here!"[3] As dawn broke in the cold morning hours of April 19, the British advance led by Major Pitcairn approached the Lexington green. Astride his horse, Pitcairn could see the militia gathered ahead of him on the green. "Throw down your arms! Ye villians, ye rebels," he shouted.[4] As the militia started to retreat in the face of such an overwhelming force of British troops, a shot rang out. No one knows who fired it. But it was immediately answered by puffs of smoke and the sounds of muskets firing. The British regulars started running across the green, attacking the colonial militia. Eight were killed and nine were wounded. The rest fled.

Eventually, the British regulars were ordered by their officers to regroup. They marched along the road to Concord, led by Colonel Smith. By this time, however, Concord had been warned that the British were approaching. Although Revere had been captured by a British patrol, another rider, Dr. Samuel Prescott, had ridden to Concord with the news. Nevertheless, the British continued their march.

Meanwhile, the colonial militia had taken up a position on Punkatesset Hill, which overlooked the North Bridge across the Concord River. The British had to cross over the bridge to reach the storehouse where they believed the colonials had stored the gunpowder and other military supplies. What the British did not know was that the military supplies had been removed from Concord before their march had even begun. The colonial leaders, fearing that Gage might try to capture them, had removed some of the supplies on April 18. On the morning of April 19, as the colonials were warned that the British were approaching, they hastily removed the rest.

> Powder was hauled into the woods and hidden. A plow was got out, furrows were struck in a near-by field; light cannon and muskets were laid in them, and other furrows covered them up.[5]

The militia moved down from the hill and advanced toward the bridge. On the other side was a contingent of British regulars. Suddenly, one of the British regulars fired at the militia. An order went out to the colonials from Major John Buttrick: "Fire, fellow soldiers; for God's sake, fire!"[6] They did. Twelve British regulars were hit. The British fled from the bridge. Colonel Smith decided not to linger any longer in Concord. The British had been unable to find any military supplies, except a few cannons. The encounter in Concord had already cost them nine casualties. So Smith reformed his troops and began to march back to Boston. It was a journey of only about 18 miles, but this retreat would be one of the most difficult that the British regulars had ever endured.

As the British retreated, swarms of colonial militia began to form around them. Having been warned that the British regulars were out in Lexington and Concord, militia from the surrounding towns had answered the call. As one British officer recalled:

> We were fired on from all sides, but mostly from the rear, where people had hid themselves in houses till we passed and then fired. The country was an amazing strong one, full of hills, woods, stone walls, etc, which the rebels did not fail to take advantage of, for they were all lined with people who kept up an incessant fire upon us, as we did too upon them but not with the same advantage, for they were so concealed there was hardly any seeing them.[7]

British troops attempted to cross the bridge leading to Concord, hoping to capture American gunpowder and other military supplies. American militiamen, who had already moved most of the supplies out of Concord, succeeded in beating off the invaders.

Indeed, the British could see only puffs of smoke as the gunpowder in the militiamen's muskets was ignited, sending lead balls flying. Many of these colonials were good marksmen, who had trained themselves by hunting in the woods. Others had fought during the French and Indian War. There were more than two thousand of them firing against the British.

The British, led by Major Pitcairn, retreated to Lexington. Here they were joined by reinforcements that Governor Gage had sent out from Boston. The retreat continued, but the pressure from the colonial militia did not let up. The colonials, directed by General William Heath, had formed skirmish lines on all sides of the British. As the enemy moved, the militia moved with them. They were firing from

As they retreated from Concord, British troops were attacked from all sides by colonial marksmen. The marksmen, who were skilled hunters familiar with the terrain, concealed themselves behind boulders and stone walls for protection. During this first true battle of the Revolutionary War, the British suffered 300 casualties.

the front, the flanks, and the rear. Shots were hitting their marks as red uniforms crumpled and fell to the ground. The British tried to retaliate. They charged some of the walls where the colonials were hidden. They shot and bayoneted some of the enemy. But very few of the colonial militia were killed or wounded.

Eventually, the British reached the safety of Boston. They had suffered 300 casualties in an attempt to capture the powder held by the colonials at Concord. The American Revolution had begun, and gunpowder had helped to start it.

2

Early Methods of Warfare

Gunpowder was essential for soldiers fighting in the American Revolution as well as in all other wars of the past 500 years. Before the use of gunpowder became common in fifteenth century Europe, however, warfare was much different. To fully understand the significance of how gunpowder changed warfare, it is important to understand the way wars were fought in the Middle Ages and even earlier. During the Middle Ages (500–1500), wars were often fought over strongholds. These were usually stone castles or towns. Much of medieval warfare consisted of sieges—that is, attacking and defending these fortresses. Siege engines, like catapults, were used to batter down the stone walls.

Armies also met on battlefields. There were clashes between small forces of mounted knights with swords and lances. However, infantry were far more numerous in these medieval armies. They fought with bows and arrows, spears and daggers.

At sea, battles occurred that were similar to those fought on land. Enemy ships would draw close, and archers aboard the ships would fire at each other. Then the ships would grapple together, and infantry from one ship would cross over to another and begin an attack. These methods of warfare, begun in the ancient world, continued throughout the Middle Ages.

WARFARE DURING THE ROMAN EMPIRE

In A.D. 69, Roman armies laid siege to the walled city of Jerusalem, the capital of Judea, because the Jews had risen in revolt against Rome. Titus, the Roman general in command,

During the Middle Ages, wars were often fought for control of stone castles or fortresses. This fifteenth century illustration shows French and Scots soldiers capturing Wark Castle in Northumberland, England.

ordered that a wall four and one-half miles in length be built around the city. He also constructed 13 forts outside the city to prevent any relief force from getting into Jerusalem. The massive wall and the forts also made it impossible for the Jews to get food into the city and people began to starve.

Hadrian's Wall, built by Emperor Hadrian in the second century, was more than 73 miles long. The Romans, who often built walls to defend their frontiers from invaders, had it built to protect their colonies in England from the attacks of fierce Celtic tribesmen.

As one contemporary, named Josephus, wrote:

The famine became more intense and devoured whole houses and families. The roofs were covered with women and babes, the streets full of old men already dead. Young men and boys swollen with hunger haunted the squares like ghosts and fell wherever faintness overcame them. To bury their kinsfolk was beyond the strength of the sick, and those who were fit shirked the task because of the number of the dead and uncertainty of their own fate; for many while burying others fell dead themselves, and many set out for their graves before their hour struck.[8]

Eventually, Jerusalem fell to the Romans.

What Josephus described was a method of warfare that existed in the ancient world and throughout the Middle Ages. The Romans and other ancient peoples built walled cities for defense. In fact, the Romans even used walls to defend their frontiers from invasion. In England, for example, a wall was built by the emperor Hadrian between A.D. 122 and 136. Called Hadrian's Wall, it stretched for over 73 miles across northern England. It was built to protect the frontier and Roman towns from invasion by local tribesmen known as Celts. Roman soldiers manned the wall until the fourth century.

By that time, the Roman Empire was collapsing. Its defenses were under enormous pressure from local tribes, such as the Visigoths, the Goths, and the Huns.

In 410, Rome itself was overrun by the Visigoths. Later in the century, another tribe, called the Ostrogoths, conquered Italy.

These tribes, however, did not change the methods of warfare. They took over the Roman towns, strengthened their defenses, and defended them. Without a unified empire, Europe broke down into a series of small, fortified areas. These included towns and forts, controlled by local rulers. These strongholds were used to defend their territories.

Inside each stronghold, the local townspeople were organized for defense in case an enemy appeared at the gates. The ruler also kept a small army of paid professionals at his command. These could march out from the stronghold and attack an enemy who might be invading his territory.

WARFARE DURING THE MIDDLE AGES

During much of the Middle Ages, castles were built according to a pattern known as motte and bailey. The motte was a mound or hill. A tower was built on top of the hill to command the countryside. A wall was erected to defend the tower, and outside the wall was a ditch called a moat. Beyond this were other buildings, the bailey, surrounded by another wall and moat. Thus, the castle had two lines of defense against attackers. Defenders could move along the walls, from one area to another, wherever the attack was strongest.

To defend the walls, soldiers relied on a variety of weapons. Infantry used bows and arrows. For centuries, they used a short bow. This was about four feet long and made of wood. It could fire an arrow with great accuracy about 100 yards. During the Middle Ages, infantry also began to use the longbow. It was approximately six feet long. A bowman pulled the string back, approximately to his ear, and arrows could be shot with accuracy over a range of about 200 yards. An expert bowman could shoot as many as five arrows per minute.

Another weapon used by the infantry was the crossbow, developed during ancient times. A horizontal bow was attached to a handle. The bowman drew a string back to a catch, called a nut. Then he pulled a trigger and let the arrow fly. The crossbow could accurately hit a target approximately 60 yards away. But it was much slower than the longbow. A crossbow could fire only about one arrow per minute. In addition to these weapons, infantry also relied on iron swords, battle-axes and knives.

To protect themselves, soldiers wore shirts of chain mail, a garment of fine metal links strung together to provide protective

This engraving depicts a knight aiming his crossbow, an important weapon used by the infantry during the Middle Ages. Knights could fire an arrow a minute, and the arrow could hit a target 60 yards away with great accuracy.

armor. Underneath the mail shirts, the soldiers also wore cotton pads. As the longbow became more widely used in the later Middle Ages, the chain mail no longer provided enough protection. The power of the longbow could drive an arrow right through the mail. For better protection, soldiers began to wear plate armor. This armor was expensive and only well-to-do knights and nobles could afford it. Eventually, soldiers began to wear full-armored suits, including helmets, breast plates, and armor over their legs. Medieval fighting men generally relied on the same weapons and dressed in the same armor for protection, whether they were defending a castle or attacking it.

As historian Terrence Wise has written, there were generally four ways for an army to capture a castle. An attacking army could try to starve it into surrender, as the Romans did against Jerusalem. The army could mount an assault over the walls or create a breech or hole in a wall and attack through it. An army could also mine walls and force them to collapse.[9]

Besieging armies generally carried siege engines. These were also used by the defenders inside the walls. They were the early versions of artillery, before the invention of gunpowder. Siege engines had been built by armies in the ancient world and continued to be used by medieval forces. One of these siege engines was the ballista, or espringale. This was a giant crossbow that fired a large arrow. The arrow could batter down the gate of a castle, make a hole in the castle wall, or kill defenders inside.

Another giant weapon was the mangonel, or catapult. One end of a large wooden beam was connected to ropes. The ropes were tightened and the beam was drawn back and hooked. A large rock weighing as much as 300 pounds was then lifted into a big wooden cup at the hooked end. Then the beam was released and sprung forward until it hit a padded cross bar. The stone was hurled forward from the cup into the air against a castle. A variation of the catapult was the trebuchet. It had a bucket at one end that was used to launch stones. By repeatedly hurling stones against the same area in a castle wall, a besieging army might eventually produce a hole. Soldiers could charge through it and capture the castle.

Rocks were also hurled into the moat surrounding a castle, creating a bridge for the besieging army to cross. Some armies built huge towers that could be rolled across a moat, allowing them to approach the castle wall. Soldiers in these towers could then lower a bridge and advance onto the castle walls.

Another method of attacking a castle was to have miners dig tunnels under the castle walls. These tunnels were strengthened by wooden beams. Once a mine was completed, piles of wood were brought into it and set on fire. The wooden beams collapsed and this would bring the castle wall tumbling down. The opening would provide an opportunity for an army to attack and overcome the defenders.

During the Middle Ages, castle defenses became stronger and stronger. Some engineers designed entire castles within castles to improve defense. Newer defenses also included flanking towers that projected outward instead of being even with the walls. These towers were built at short intervals along the length of a wall. Archers could fire from the towers in two directions. Slits made in the walls allowed the archers to see the enemy as they fired their arrows while they remained hidden and protected from enemy arrows. Towns in Europe began to develop similar defenses to protect their citizens from invasion.

These defenses sprang up not only in Europe but also in the Middle East. During the seventh century, an Arab prophet named Muhammad founded a new religion called Islam. Following his death, Muslim soldiers began conquering vast territories to spread Islam across the Middle East and northern Africa. Eventually, they captured Jerusalem, a city sacred to the Muslims, who believed it was the place from which Muhammad rose into heaven. It was also sacred to Christians who believed that it was the place where Jesus Christ died and ascended into heaven.

In the eleventh century, the Christian leaders of Europe launched a Crusade designed to recapture Jerusalem. The Crusade was called by Pope Urban II, the spiritual head of Christian Europe. Eventually, Jerusalem was besieged and captured by the Crusaders in 1099. The Crusaders established Christian kingdoms in the Middle East, but these came under immediate attack from the Muslims. At one siege, described by a Muslim soldier, Usamah Ibn-Munqidh, many of the classic techniques of siege warfare were used, including mining. After the tunnel was complete, the Arab miners "began to cut dry wood and stuff the tunnel with it. Early the next morning they set it on fire. We had just at that time put on our arms and marched. . . . As soon as the fire began to have its effect, the layers of mortar between the stones of the wall began to fall. Then a crack was made. The crack became wider and wider and the tower fell." [10]

Once the tower collapsed, the Muslims attacked. The Christians defended the tower with arrows. A band of Christians remained on one part of the tower. One of the Muslims "climbed, under our very eyes, and started walking towards the tower, in the face of death, until he approached and hurled a bottle of naphtha on those who were on top of it. The naphtha flashed like a meteor falling upon those hard stones, while the men who were there threw themselves on the ground for fear of being burnt." [11] Eventually the castle fell to the Muslims.

Naphtha, described here, was a weapon widely used throughout the Middle Ages. It was often called "Greek fire" because it had first been developed by the ancient Greeks. The so-called "Greek fire" consisted of a mixture of naphtha (petroleum), sulfur, and oil taken from the resin of trees. As historian J.R. Partington wrote: "The Greek fire was used by special 'naphtha troops' attached to each corps of archers in the Muslim army . . . who wore fireproof suits and threw incendiary material." [12] Greek fire was poured into small containers, which were thrown like modern hand grenades. Archers dipped their arrows in Greek fire and fired them during sieges. The arrows might then set wooden buildings ablaze inside the enemy castle.

Greek fire was also used in naval battles. It was placed in long tubes and pumped through them, sending a wall of fire against an enemy ship. In most naval battles, however, men

In 1340, the great naval battle of Sluys was fought between France and England. Archers on each side shot deadly arrows from their crossbows. As the enemy ships drew closer together, men-at-arms fought hand-to-hand with swords, knives, and battleaxes.

fought in hand-to-hand combat with swords, knives, and battle-axes as if they were attacking and defending a castle. A typical naval battle was fought between French and English fleets at Sluys off the coast of France in 1340.

As described by one British writer, Geoffrey Le Baker: "An iron cloud of bolts from crossbows, and arrows from bows, fell upon [the French] bringing death to thousands. Then those who wished, or were daring enough, came to blows at close quarters with spears, pikes, and swords; stones, thrown from the ships' castles, also killed many. In brief, this was without a doubt an important and terrible battle. . . ."[13]

The French were eventually defeated with losses that may have reached as high as 18,000 men.

MEDIEVAL BATTLEFIELDS

Cavalry has often been considered the most important military force on medieval battlefields. Medieval poets wrote about armored knights charging the enemy and winning important battles. These same knights were glorified in songs for their courage and their chivalry. Modern historians, however, have discovered that the reality of medieval battles was quite different. In the typical army of the Middle Ages, there were five or six times the number of infantry as cavalry.

Although knights and archers might ride to the battlefield, they then dismounted and fought on foot. It was difficult for archers to shoot from the saddle until the stirrup became widely used by about A.D. 1000. Stirrups enabled soldiers to keep themselves on a horse without holding on to the reins. This left their hands free to shoot their bows. Meanwhile, saddles added a brace at the back. This enabled a knight to use a lance against his enemy without being pushed out of the saddle.

Cavalry used a variety of weapons, including the sword, the axe, and the lance. A lance was a long spear, about 12 to 14 inches long, with a metal point. Mounted knights might also use a mace—a club with a head that had metal spikes in it. The cavalry included knights on armored horses and men of lower rank called sergeants who rode smaller horses. Squires served the knights in battle. These were often young men or boys who had not yet become knights. Their responsibility included dressing the knight in his armor before the battle and carrying extra weapons if the knight lost his sword or lance during combat. They were also expected to fight, if necessary, when the knights were outnumbered.

The infantry, however, were the mainstay of the army. They were organized into companies. In France, there were 25 to 30 men in each company. They included spearmen, and men with crossbows. In England, the infantry companies included archers with longbows. These archers proved to be decisive during several of the battles of the Hundred Years' War (1337–1453). This war was fought over territory in France that was claimed by the English king. In 1346, England's King Edward III met the

Battle of Hastings

Cavalry, combined with infantry, could prove decisive in a medieval battle. An example was the Battle of Hastings, fought in 1066. Earlier that year Harold Godwinson, Earl of Wessex, had been declared king following the death of his friend, King Edward. However, William of Normandy claimed that he had been promised the throne. William led an invading force from France and met Harold on the battlefield of Hastings, in southern England on October 14.

Harold had taken up a strong position on a hill with his army of about 8,000 men. William advanced with a force of 10,000, including about 3,000 cavalry. These horsemen knew better than to charge against Harold's infantry who were armed with long spears that could easily knock the knights out of their saddles. At first William's bowmen fired their arrows against Harold's position, hoping to kill as many men as possible. But Harold's men held firm. Then William's cavalry pretended to leave the battle-field as if the army had been beaten. Some of Harold's men left their position to chase after them. William's cavalry turned and cut down the enemy while they were advancing in a disorganized group. Meanwhile, William's infantry advanced against Harold's remaining forces on the hill. Harold was struck by an arrow and killed. William won the battle and became king of England. To this day he is known as William the Conqueror.

French knights at the Battle of Crecy. The king's archers cut down the knights by shooting at their horses. This helped to decide the outcome of the battle. The English repeated their victory 10 years later at the Battle of Poitiers. Perhaps the most remarkable English victory occurred at Agincourt in northeastern France on October 25, 1415, the Feast of St. Crispin. King Henry V of England led about 6,000 men, mostly archers, against a French force five times larger. In his play *Henry V,* William Shakespeare has King Henry address his men shortly before the battle begins:

> We few, we happy few, we band of brothers;
> For he today that sheds his blood with me
> Shall be my brother; be he ne'er so vile,
> This day shall gentle his condition:
> And gentlemen in England now a-bed
> Shall think themselves accursed they were not here,
> And hold their manhoods cheap whiles any speaks
> That fought with us upon Saint Crispin's day.
> [*Henry V,* Act 4, Scene 3]

This time, many of the French knights were dismounted, having learned from earlier battles not to ride toward the English archers. Instead they slowly advanced on foot, burdened with heavy armor, against the English lines. Later, a French knight wrote,

> [The knights] were so loaded with armor that they could not support themselves or move forward. In the first place they were armed with long coats of steel, reaching to the knees or lower, and very heavy . . . and besides plate armor also most of them had hooded helmets; wherefore this weight of armor, with the softness of the wet ground, [it had rained the previous night] . . . kept them as if immovable, so that they could raise their clubs only with great difficulty. . . .[14]

By the time they reached the English lines, many of the French knights were hit by arrows. Those knights who fought hand-to-hand with the English were tired. They were also packed so tightly together in such a small area on the battlefield that it was difficult for them to raise their weapons. The archers grabbed swords from the wounded knights who had fallen to the ground and struck down those who were still standing. The archers then took out their knives and cut open the helmets of the knights, killing those who had fallen and could not get up because of their heavy armor. Thousands were slaughtered.[15]

In addition to the English longbow, infantrymen also used the pike to defeat mounted knights. The pike, a long shaft 15 to 18 feet long with a metal point, was widely used by the Swiss infantry. During the fourteenth century, the Swiss were fighting for their independence against the Hapsburgs, one of the oldest and most powerful ruling families in Europe. The pike was a weapon that many citizens could afford, and because of this, the Swiss were able to create a mass infantry that used the pike in battle. A variation of the pike was the halbred. This was a long pole with a sharp metal point on the end and an axe on the side. Some infantry also carried bills. These were pikes with hooks on the side. Bills were used to pull knights out of their saddles.

During a battle, the Swiss pikemen moved quickly across a battlefield to take up a position against an enemy. In the face of a cavalry charge, they presented a forest of sharp pikes that proved devastating to armored knights. The pikemen also fought in combination with archers. By the fifteenth century, these weapons and the men who used them would begin to disappear from the battlefield.

The invention of gunpowder would make the pike, the longbow, the catapult and the armored knight obsolete. Castles and walled cities would often prove impossible to defend against it. In short, gunpowder would change warfare forever.

3

Gunpowder Arrives in Europe

Gunpowder and the weapons invented to use it began to appear on European battlefields during the fourteenth century. Cannon, for example, were fired by the French at Crecy in 1346, but these early cannons were still unperfected and they had no impact on the outcome of the battle. Over the next century, however, gunpowder changed the course of military history.

Large cannon, powered by gunpowder, started to batter down the walls of cities and castles. The French used their cannons to win the Hundred Years' War by 1453. In that same year, the Ottoman Turks brought their cannons to the walls of Constantinople and captured it.

On the battlefield, hand cannon (also known as arquebuses) were used by European infantry. Arquebuses proved more powerful than bows and arrows or pikes. As a result, armies using these new weapons began to win decisive victories. Meanwhile, on the high seas, a combination of the cannon and the arquebus revolutionized warfare, leading to new naval tactics and the destruction of enemy fleets at battles such as the one fought at Lepanto in 1571. By 1600, gunpowder had become an essential matériel (military equipment) of war for the armies and navies of Europe.

INTRODUCTION OF GUNPOWDER

Gunpowder probably originated in China. Historian Jixing Pan wrote that in the eleventh century the Chinese already had the ingredients of gunpowder. They were using it for rockets and

Cannon began to appear on European battlefields during the fourteenth century. But as this painting of the Battle of Crecy shows, hand-to-hand combat and huge rocks hurled by catapults were still important tactics used in warfare.

fireworks by the twelfth century.[16] In addition, the Chinese used Greek fire and flaming arrows against their enemies.

In Europe, a formula for gunpowder was discovered by an English scientist named Roger Bacon. Born in 1214, Bacon attended Oxford University outside of London. Later he taught at Oxford and became an expert in alchemy. This was the practice, carried on by some Medieval scientists, of trying to produce gold out of other metals. During his work in the laboratory, Bacon mixed together sulfur, charcoal, and saltpeter. Suddenly, the pot that contained them exploded.

Bacon realized that he had invented something with enormous potential for destruction. As he wrote, "thus you can make thunder and lightning, if you know the means." Later, about 1267, he went beyond his earlier observation: "No clap of thunder can compare with such noises. Some of them strike such terror to the sight that the thunders and lightnings of the clouds disturb it considerably less." Finally, Bacon wrote that while he had discovered something that was currently only a "child's toy," if it were enclosed in "an instrument . . . made of solid material the violence of the explosion would be much greater." [17]

Gunpowder consists of 75 percent saltpeter, 12.5 percent sulfur, and 12.5 percent charcoal. During the late Medieval period, saltpeter, or potassium nitrate, was produced from animal manure and urine. The saltpeter had to be separated from the waste products, then purified. Charcoal was produced by burning a mound of wood. Finally, the sulfur was dug from various mines in Europe.

At first the ingredients were mixed together by a worker using a large mortar (a thick bowl) and pestle (a long tool, shaped like a club, used for grinding). Gradually, machines were developed that could produce larger amounts of gunpowder far more rapidly. During the fifteenth century, a process known as corning was invented. Before corning, gunpowder was finely powdered and burned too slowly. It lacked power. The corning process created individual grains of gunpowder. These were produced by forcing the gunpowder through a series of sieves with holes to create the granular powder. [18] As a result, the gunpowder burned faster and became more powerful. Corning also reduced the amount of moisture absorbed by gunpowder.

This was a serious problem that could spoil the powder. Before corning, gunpowder makers added a little vinegar to the gunpowder to create powder loaves. This tightly packed powder was easier to transport and far more resistant to moisture and spoilage.[19] Later, gunpowder was usually transported in barrels. These were made of wood and metal. Gunpowder was also carried in cans or boxes. Gunpowder remained stable in these containers. Once it was ignited, however, the powder would explode.

Of course, gunpowder by itself was not enough to transform warfare. It had to be combined with weapons that could use the power of burning gunpowder. When gunpowder burns, it produces a gas that expands. If the expanding gas is contained in a cylinder, like a cannon, it will drive a cannon ball through the open end of the cannon at a high speed. Gunpowder is known as a *propellant*. The cannon ball is called *ammunition*.

Iron and brass cannon began to be produced in Europe during the fourteenth century. These cannon were made from long metal strips, bound together by metal hoops. The early cannon were primitive. They did not have any wheels. Instead they were tied to the trunks of trees and hauled in front of walled cities. The tree trunks were dug into the ground to give the cannon a stable position when it was fired. The recoil—or jolt backward—when a cannon shot a projectile or ammunition forward was tremendous.

The earliest projectiles were metal arrows. The arrows were aimed at the doors of castles and fired from short distances. If the force was powerful enough, it would knock down the castle door and an attacking army could enter the castle. In addition to arrows, the cannon shot stones. These were hurled against castle walls or shot over the walls and landed on buildings inside. One enormous cannon developed in France during the fifteenth century was called "Mons Meg." It weighed 15 tons and hurled an 18-inch granite ball against a target. It took 100 men to pull "Mons Meg" along on its wheels. But it was very effective at knocking down the walls of enemy strongholds.[20]

These early cannon were called bombards. They could be loaded from the front, or muzzle. Cannon were also loaded from the rear, or breech. A charge of powder was added at the rear of the cannon, then lit to ignite the charge and fire the ammunition. Stones were soon replaced as ammunition by iron balls that could do even more damage. But the early cannon were frequently unreliable. The gun barrels were also caked with gunpowder after they were fired and had to be cleaned following each firing. Once when a Scottish king was inspecting his guns during a siege, one of them blew up while firing and killed him.

During the fifteenth century, new inventions in artillery began to appear. These included case, canister and grape shot. Case shot consists of small stones and nails in a case. When it is fired, the stones and nails break out of the case and can hit a number of enemy soldiers. The canister works in much the same way, using a container filled with small balls. Grape is a bag with small shot in it. Each of these projectiles was used on the battlefield against infantry. By 1500, cannon could hit targets at about 200 yards and fire about four times per hour.[21] This was extremely slow, but when the target was hit, the result could be devastating.

As large cannon were being developed, smaller guns that could be carried by infantrymen were also being produced. These were known as small bombards or hand culverins. They were metal tubes attached to a piece of wood or metal. Each one weighed approximately 10 pounds. A soldier used a match to light the gunpowder in the rear of the tube. It then fired a metal bullet toward the enemy. Frequently the handgun rested on a metal support that a soldier could push into the ground.

Guns were first used in Germany during the last part of the fourteenth century. They were not always reliable. A club or battleaxe was often attached to one end. If the gun did not work, a soldier could defend himself with a battleaxe. Some guns had to be operated by two soldiers. According to historian

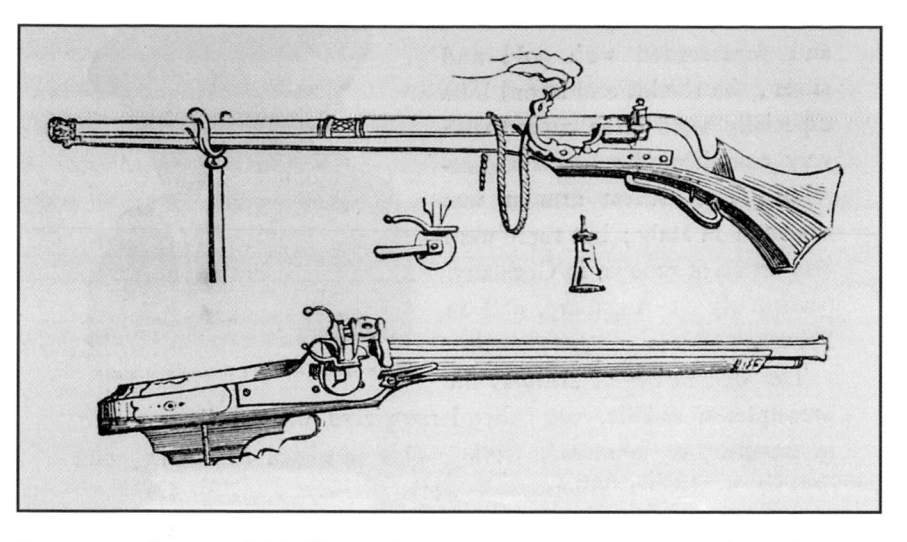

The gun at the top of this illustration weighed almost 10 pounds and had to be propped up by a metal support. The powder was kept in a pan and was lit by a piece of cotton treated with gunpowder. Two infantrymen often had to work together to fire it. The gun shown below, an arquebus, was much easier to use because a trigger ignited the gunpowder.

W.W. Greener, "One man . . . leveled and held the weapon during discharge, [and] his companion . . . applied the priming and the match [adding the powder and lighting it] and assisted in loading and carrying the weapon."[22] Hand culverins ranged from four to eight feet in length.

Initially, the powder in a pan at the rear of a gun was lit by a "match"—a piece of cotton treated with gunpowder. This was extremely difficult for a lone soldier, who was also trying to hold and aim the gun. As a result, two infantrymen had to work together. During the latter part of the fifteenth century, however, the matchlock was invented in Germany. The matchlock gun was much easier to operate. The matchlock was a piece of S-shaped metal that held a lit "match" in an upright position. By means of a trigger, a soldier could bring the piece of metal downward with the lit match to ignite the gunpowder in the pan.

These matchlocks were incorporated into a new type of gun, called an arquebus. Eventually, in the sixteenth century, the matchlock was replaced by a wheel lock. This device was a metal wheel with teeth. The wheel could be turned by the trigger, producing sparks when it rubbed against another piece of metal over the pan. In this way, the gunpowder was ignited.

Comparing the arquebus to the longbow, historian Terrence Wise wrote: "the handgun of the late fifteenth century had the advantage of being easy to use once a man had been trained; anyone could be trained in a few weeks and hand gunners did not need great strength and constant practice as did the longbow man." The arquebus also packed as much power as the longbow. However, a soldier could only fire eight shots an hour, while the longbow could fire five arrows per minute. [23]

IMPACT OF GUNPOWDER

Nevertheless, gunpowder and the weapons that used it gradually replaced all other weapons over the next two centuries. The first impact of gunpowder was felt in sieges of castles and walled cities. The French were among the earliest to use cannon. It was very effective during the last part of the Hundred Years' War and helped to drive the English out of France. Most of the cities that the English had captured fell to the French. For example, the city of Harfleur, wrote one historian, "which had resisted a siege for six weeks in 1415, and for six months in 1440, fell to Charles VII of France in December 1449 after only 17 days thanks to the damage inflicted by the 16 bombards [developed] specially for this task." Seventy other English cities and castles were also captured by the French king between 1449 and 1450. And the French artillery played a key part in many of these victories.[24]

Cannon could knock down the high walls of cities and castles. As a result, military leaders soon began to develop defenses against them. One obvious defense was to place cannon inside the walls of a city where they could shoot back at the besiegers. The walls themselves were also changed. High walls were replaced by shorter, squatter, thicker walls that were harder to knock down. This new kind of defense was first developed in Italy. Italian city-states were constantly battling each other for control of territory. To defend themselves they began to build new types of walls to protect their cities. The Italian architects who designed these defenses traveled to other parts of Europe where they built similar fortifications.

Beyond the walls, Italian military engineers also erected defensive works that projected far outward. These were sometimes placed on the far side of a moat from the main castle walls. Called crownworks and hornworks, they were armed with cannon. The castle cannon could fire at enemy besiegers and keep their cannon out of range of the main walls of a town or castle.

As these new defenses developed during the sixteenth century, warfare changed. Sieges took much longer than they had earlier when besiegers had the advantage with their cannon. Warfare also began to become far more expensive. Great amounts of money had to be spent to fortify cities and purchase cannon. Bigger armies were also necessary and far more expensive to put in the field or to defend a fortified position.[25]

Building defenses took time. Meanwhile, the besiegers maintained an advantage over the defenders of a fortified position. This was demonstrated in 1453, when the Ottoman Turks lay siege to the city of Constantinople in Asia Minor. This city had been founded by the Roman emperor Constantine in the fourth century A.D. on the site of another city called Byzantium. Constantinople became the capitol of a large Byzantine Empire that remained powerful throughout the Middle Ages.

During the fourteenth and fifteenth centuries, however, the Ottoman Turks began to build an enormous empire that stretched across Asia Minor and into the Balkans. The Turks took over much of the territory that had formed part of the Byzantine Empire. Constantinople became more and more isolated. Nevertheless, it occupied a strong defensive position. Constantinople was located on a peninsula along the Bosphorus.

This is a narrow strait that separates the Adriatic Sea from the Black Sea. An enemy force would have to lay siege to the city both by land and sea to conquer it.

During the fifteenth century, an Ottoman Sultan—or king—named Mehmed II decided that his armies were strong enough to capture Constantinople and put an end to the Byzantine Empire.

Mehmed II

As a child in Turkey, Mehmed was not considered a likely candidate to become king. He had two older brothers, one of whom was expected to succeed their father as sultan. Mehmed was not interested in receiving the education necessary for a position in the Turkish government. Mehmed's brothers, however, died when they were still very young. As a result, at the age of 11, Mehmed found himself heir to his father's throne. His father immediately ordered Mehmed to pay better attention to his education and assigned a new teacher to him. "Your father has sent me to instruct you," the teacher told him, "but also to keep you in order if you refuse to obey."*

In 1451, when his father died, Mehmed succeeded him as sultan and officially became known as Mehmed II. One of his first goals as a new sultan was to capture Constantinople. Constantinople had withstood several sieges over the past one thousand years. But Mehmed, who was dedicated to consolidating the power of the Turks in the area, was convinced that he could succeed where others had failed. Mehmed believed that a siege cannon could help him achieve his goal. Therefore he hired a Hungarian engineer named Urban, an artillery expert, to build a large number of cannon. The largest was over 26 feet long and shot a cannonball that weighed 1,200 pounds.**

Mehmed was obsessed with the upcoming siege of Constantinople. "Sleepless, he would spend all night poring over drawings of its defenses, planning his lines of attack, the position to be occupied by his troops, the emplacements of his ... batteries...."***

* Lord Kinross, *The Ottoman Centuries: The Rise and Fall of the Turkish Empire* (New York: Morrow, 1977), 88.

**Ibid., 99.

***Ibid., 99–100.

The sultan put together an enormous army of 100,000 men, troops armed with artillery, and a magnificent fleet, and the siege of Constantinople began in April 1453. Mehmed's soldiers fired their artillery at the walls of Constantinople. In many places, large holes were created and the Turks tried to enter the city through them. But they were pushed back, and the defenders repaired the walls of the city. The siege continued until May 29, 1453. On this day, the sultan's artillery began an enormous barrage against the city, led by the enormous gun designed by Urban. It created a huge opening in the defenses of Constantinople. The Turks attacked and a furious hand-to-hand struggle occurred for control of the defense works. One of the Byzantine leaders was killed. As a result, the defenders lost heart and began to retreat. The Turks were victorious and took control of the city. It became their new capital and was renamed Istanbul.

Constantinople was not the only battle where cannon and gunpowder had played an important role. During the latter fifteenth century, the Spanish were trying to drive the Muslims, called Moors, out of Spain. The Muslims had invaded the country during the eighth century, pushing the Christian forces into northern Spain. Over the next seven centuries, however, the Christians gradually drove back the Moors until they occupied only a small kingdom called Granada in southern Spain. During the late fifteenth century the Spanish monarchs Ferdinand and Isabella vowed to push the remaining Moors out of Spain. Ferdinand used artillery to batter down the Moorish defenses. At one siege, he used large iron tubes carried on carts that shot cannon balls against a Moorish stronghold. Eventually, with the help of his cannon, Ferdinand drove out the Moors in 1492.

Gunpowder, along with cannon, had also appeared on battlefields. In 1450, the French used cannon against the English at the battle of Formigny. The cannon tore huge holes in the lines of English archers. The archers attacked and tried to capture the guns, but they were defeated by the more heavily armored French infantry.

During the fifteenth century, England was being torn apart by a civil war called the War of the Roses. It was fought between two groups of nobles, the House of York and the House of Lancaster. At the battle of Barnet in 1471, the Lancastrians used cannon against the camp of the Yorkists. However, the Lancastrians were using the new corned gunpowder, which was more powerful than the old powder they were accustomed to. Thus, the cannon balls were fired over the Yorkist camp and did not kill any of the enemy. In the morning, smoke from the gunpowder, which had been fired through the night, covered the battlefield. When the Lancastrians charged, they lost sight of each other and began killing their own men. As a result, the Yorkists won a decisive victory.

In 1515, French artillery faced an army of Swiss pikemen at the battle of Marignano in Italy, just south of the Swiss Alps. As the pikemen advanced they were struck by cannon balls from the French artillery. Nevertheless, the pikeman kept charging toward the guns trying to silence them. During the charge, they were attacked by French cavalry and decisively defeated. This was the first time that pikemen had been beaten by gunpowder and artillery.

In Italy, other changes were also occurring on the battle-field. Italian city-states began using a combination of pikemen and arquebusiers in battle. These infantry soldiers were very effective in winning victories. Indeed, they often proved to be too powerful for cavalry to defeat them. New infantry formations also began to appear in other parts of Europe. One reason for the spread of this type of warfare was printing. During the fifteenth century, printing had begun to appear in Germany. Printing presses meant that books could be produced more cheaply and in much greater quantity than those produced by hand. In the past, books had to be copied, which took many hours and meant that very few books were produced. The printing press allowed military writers to describe the infantry formations used on the battlefields. These could then be read by military leaders in other parts of Europe, who adopted them in their own armies.

During the sixteenth century, the military leaders of Europe recognized how much gunpowder was transforming warfare. It was replacing the longbow, the sword, and even the pike. Europe's nobility, who led the armies, began to incorporate cannon not only in their war machines but also in their daily lives. As historian Thomas Arnold wrote: "In peacetime as well as in war, cannon salutes—from forts, from ships at sea, from armies in review—added a . . . deeply impressive flourish and flash to arrivals and departures, births and weddings, and other great moments in the lives of the powerful." [29]

In naval battles, artillery and handguns were combined to create a new type of warfare. At Lepanto near Greece in 1571, Turkish and Christian navies relied on huge galleys that were rowed into battle. The Christian navy also included several galleasses—ships that were rowed and also had sails. Both sides used cannon to fire against each other. The galleasses were more heavily armed with cannon. They fired against the Turkish galleys, which began to fall out of their tight formation and lose the battle. In the meantime, there were fierce fights between individual ships on each side. Arquebusiers fired at each other from the ships. Eventually, the Turkish commander was killed by a bullet from an enemy arquebus. His ship was captured by the Christians who won the battle.

Lepanto was a decisive naval victory for the Christians against the Muslim Turks. It was also the first major naval battle won with gunpowder. Up until this time, the Turks had been the dominant sea power in much of the Mediterranean Sea. "After Lepanto," wrote one historian, "the Ottoman navy never recovered its earlier near mastery of the Mediterranean. . . ." [30]

Gradually the number of cannon on the ships increased, and naval tactics changed. Naval captains were advised that

In 1571, Turkish and Christian navies fought a fierce battle at Lepanto. Both sides had huge galleys (ships with oars and sails) and cannon. After the Turkish commander was killed by a bullet from an arquebus, the Turks lost the battle. They also lost control of the Mediterranean Sea.

"you are not to come to close quarters with them [the enemy] if you can avoid it, but only with your artillery are you to compel them to strike sail . . . so that . . . war may be waged with greater safety, and so that less loss may result to the people of your ships."[31]

In general, the coming of gunpowder had helped spark what historians have called a revolution in military warfare during the sixteenth century. Sieges, battlefield encounters, and naval engagements were now completely different from those of earlier times.

4

The Conquest of Empires

AT ISSUE

During the fifteenth and sixteenth centuries, European nations along the Atlantic Ocean sent out their sailing ships to the East Indies and the New World. Explorers from Spain and Portugal, France and England hoped to discover rich treasures of gold and silver. They also wanted to take control of the trade in spices. In the past, the spice trade had been in the hands of the Muslims and the Italian city-states. They brought spices, such as pepper and cinnamon, overland from the Orient to Europe.

With their sailing ships armed with cannon, the Portuguese sailed to the East Indies and established a large trading empire there. In the New World, Spanish conquistadors conquered the vast empires of the Aztecs in Mexico and the Incas in South America. The Spaniards used cannon and arquebuses (also called muskets) to help them make their conquests. In North America, the French and the English used gunpowder to win their early victories over the Native Americans.

Meanwhile, in Europe, gunpowder was changing the ways that armies engaged in battle and tried to win large continental empires. During the seventeenth century, muskets were improved. Generals also developed new tactics to use artillery and muskets more effectively.

PORTUGAL ESTABLISHES AN EMPIRE

Born in 1394, Prince Henry of Portugal became the leader of Portuguese efforts to establish an overseas empire during the fifteenth century. When he was still in his twenties, Henry

PRINCE HENRY
OF
PORTUGALL

CEUTA

Prince Henry the Navigator led Portugal's efforts to establish an empire during the fifteenth century. As a young man, Henry built a naval station from which Portuguese ships sailed to Africa and India, beginning a lucrative trade in gold, slaves, and exotic spices. Later, Portuguese explorers ventured as far as South America, conquering and colonizing vast territories.

established a naval station called Sagres on the south coast of Portugal. From Sagres he sent out sailing ships to explore the coast of Africa.

These sailing ships were much heavier than galleys and

could sail along the rough waters of the Atlantic Ocean. The ships had large square sails. Some of these heavier ships had large castles on the prow (front) and the stern (rear). There they could carry cannon. In addition, cannon could be placed on a heavy lower deck of a sailing ship and fired through portholes.

The Portuguese used their sailing ships to set up a lucrative trade with Africans in gold, slaves and other items. Although Prince Henry died in 1460, Portuguese explorations continued. Eventually, their ships rounded the tip of Africa and began sailing toward India. Led by sea captain Vasco de Gama, the Portuguese reached India in 1498. They sailed into the port of Calicut on the southwest coast of India. According to one historian, the local ruler agreed to trade spices—including cloves, ginger, and pepper—with the Portuguese largely because their ships were armed with cannon.[32]

De Gama established the first Portuguese trading post at Calicut, then set sail back to Portugal. Along the way, he was attacked by Muslim ships. The Muslims had invaded India several centuries earlier and controlled much of the area. De Gama, however, used his cannon to drive back the Muslim vessels and eventually reached Portugal. After meeting with de Gama, the Portuguese king announced that he hoped the "great trade which now enriches the Moors [Muslims] shall . . . be diverted to the natives and ships of our own kingdom, so that henceforth all Christendom shall be able to provide itself with these spices. . . ."[33]

Early in the sixteenth century, more Portuguese ships arrived in India under the command of de Gama. In addition to spices, the Portuguese also began to trade for precious stones. These included diamonds, pearls, and rubies.[34] In order to keep the local rulers under control, the Portuguese sent larger fleets, heavily armed with cannon. These ships drove the Muslim traders from the trade routes. With his superior firepower, de Gama was able to patrol the Indian coast and prevent any trader from doing business there unless he had the permission of the Portuguese. Any cities that defied the Portuguese were bombarded. Portugal also established a chain of forts, bristling with cannon, to protect their trade routes.

From India, the Portuguese extended their empire to Southeast Asia. In 1511, they arrived at the port of Malacca, located in the present-day nation of Malaysia. When the local ruler refused to submit to Portuguese rule, they bombarded the city. After landing on the beaches, the Portuguese brought their cannon on shore. They "placed them so as to shoot straight down the avenues to keep the [enemy] from digging fresh trenches for defense."[35] After a fierce struggle, the Portuguese were victorious. With the aid of their gunpowder and cannon, the Portuguese established a rich empire in the East Indies.

SPAIN BRINGS GUNPOWDER TO THE AMERICAS

Portugal was not the only nation to use gunpowder successfully to overwhelm local rulers. In 1492, the Genoese navigator Christopher Columbus convinced King Ferdinand and Queen Isabella of Spain to finance a voyage to the spice islands of the east. Columbus believed that he could reach the Orient by sailing west instead of around the tip of Africa. Instead, he reached the islands of the Caribbean Sea. Here Columbus encountered a population of peaceful Indians known as Tainos. They used simple bows and arrows and had never seen weapons fired with gunpowder.

To impress them, Columbus fired off a cannon he had brought with him. As he reported, the chief was "astonished" and "when his people heard the shots they all fell to the ground."[36] Gunpowder was used to show the natives the power of the invaders.

In Mexico, however, the Spanish met a far more powerful Indian people than the Tainos. During the fourteenth century, the Aztec Indians had established their capital at Tenochtitlán in central Mexico. The city was built on an island in Lake Texcoco and was connected to the mainland by several causeways. From

Tenochtitlán, the Aztecs ruled a far-flung empire that covered much of Mexico. The tribes they conquered were forced to pay taxes to the Aztec emperor. They were also required to send a steady stream of victims who were sacrificed to the Aztec gods.

The Aztecs were successful farmers as well as gifted craftsmen, who shaped gold taken from Mexican mines into magnificent ornaments and jewelry. They controlled their empire with a powerful army. But the weapons used by their soldiers were primitive, at least by comparison to those that were being developed in Europe. The Aztecs fought with stones and slings as well as metal tipped arrows and javelins. They struck their enemies with wooden clubs reinforced with obsidian, a type of glass produced from nearby volcanoes. Aztec weapons proved to be no match for the Spaniards' steel swords, metal body armor, horses, and cannon.

In 1519, the Spaniards invaded the Aztec Empire. Spanish troops were led by a conquistador named Hernán Cortés. Born in 1485, Cortés was trained as a soldier. He sailed to the New World about 1506. Five years later, he participated in the Spanish conquest of Cuba. The governor of Cuba then ordered him to lead a small army to Mexico and establish Spanish control there.

Cortés's army consisted of approximately 500 soldiers. Over the next few years, he would face enemy armies many times this size. But his weapons gave him a distinct advantage. As one contemporary wrote, "The advantage of having horse and cannon is very necessary in this land, for it gives force and advantage to few against many."[37] Initially, Cortés encountered the Mayan Indians. They had developed a highly advanced civilization on the Yucatan peninsula in southern Mexico. In his first battle with them, Cortés "fired the cannon at the Indians, who were naturally frightened . . . for Cortés, the important lesson was that, even with these more sophisticated people, the use of guns could have a shock effect out of all proportion to their lethal consequence [killing ability]."[38] The Indians

Montezuma welcomes Hernán Cortés, the leader of the Spanish explorers, who invaded Mexico in 1519. Armed with guns and cannon, they defeated the Mayan Indians and then conquered the Aztec Empire ruled by Montezuma. The Aztec capital of Tenochtitlán was destroyed, and Spain established an empire that lasted for three centuries.

regrouped and attacked, but their arrows and obsidian swords were no match for the Spanish steel weapons. In another battle, the Spanish rode their horses into battle. The horses were also frightening to the Indians, who had never seen such animals before.

As the Spaniards traveled northward, they were met by ambassadors from the Aztec ruler, Montezuma. He had heard about the terrible cannon, which the Spanish had used in battle. Montezuma was not certain who these invaders might be. He seemed to believe that they might be gods who had come to his empire to take control of it.[39] Therefore, he decided that there was very little he could do to stop them. Meanwhile, Cortés relentlessly advanced against Tenochtitlán. Along the way, he tried to win the support of tribes that had been defeated by the Aztecs. They hated their conquerors and were eager to see them overthrown. But Cortés was not always successful in peaceful diplomacy. He also resorted to warfare. With his steel swords and armor, as well as his cannon, he overwhelmed his enemies. Some joined with him against the Aztecs, transporting supplies and hauling cannon.

Eventually, Cortés and his allies reached the capital city. Tenochtitlán was one of the largest cities in the world with more than 200,000 inhabitants. Cortés marched along one of the three causeways that connected the mainland to the city. There he met Montezuma. He "came forward on a litter [a large chair] with a canopy of green feathers and much gold and silver embroidery, and fitted with jade. It was carried by noblemen. Other noblemen busied themselves sweeping the ground in front. A man walked before the Emperor carrying a stick to mark his authority." [40]

At first, relations between Cortés and Montezuma appeared to be friendly. However, the Spanish conquistador had decided that the only way that his small army could conquer this huge empire was to control Montezuma. Cortés decided to take him hostage and run the empire using Montezuma as a Spanish puppet. The conquistador also imprisoned a number of Aztec nobles and took their families as hostages to ensure obedience. Then Cortés insisted that Montezuma have large quantities of gold delivered by his subjects from various parts of the empire to enrich the Spanish.

Although the Aztecs were upset by what Montezuma asked them to do, they followed his orders. Meanwhile, Cortés left one of his subordinates in charge of the emperor and went back to the coast to put down a revolt among some Spanish soldiers who wanted to take over his operations. When he returned to Tenochtitlán, the Aztecs were in revolt.

The Aztec revolt led to a major defeat for Cortés and his

army. But Cortés refused to give up his plans to conquer Mexico. He retreated eastward where he gathered reinforcements. Cortés also ordered his carpenters to make parts for about 12 ships. These were carried overland to Lake Texcoco. Cortés took control of the cities around the lake, assembled the ships, and launched them in April 1521. Cannon were mounted on each of the ships. With this firepower, Cortés cleared the lake of the Aztec canoes and laid siege to Technochtitlán. "As the wind was very good," he later said, "we broke through an infinite number of canoes and killed or drowned many of them [the Aztec warriors]: a most remarkable sight."[41] He also took control of the causeways, and with his cannon began to bombard the city. Eventually, the Spanish entered Technochtitlán where they fought the Aztec defenders, using their cannon to knock down the defenses. Gradually, the capital was destroyed. The Aztecs surrendered after a three-month battle.

Battle at Tenochtitlán

The revolt of the Aztecs in Tenochtitlán, an ancient Mexican city, began during May 1520. The Spanish feared that the Aztecs were preparing to rise up against them during an annual festival. To prevent the uprising, the Spanish decided to strike first. The Spanish conquistadors, led by Hernán Cortés, slaughtered hundreds of Aztec nobles who were participating in the festivities. This infuriated the Aztecs who revolted against the Spanish. Montezuma, the ruler of the Aztecs, was ordered by the conquistadors to speak to his people and persuade them to put down their arms. Many of the Aztecs stopped fighting, but only temporarily. After Cortés returned, the revolt broke out again. Once again Montezuma asked his people to stop fighting, but they stoned him. Soon afterward, he died, probably from his wounds. Cortés realized that he must retreat from Tenochtitlán. Without the authority of Montezuma, no Spaniard was safe. The Spanish began to slip out of the city during the night of July 1, 1520. But their retreat was discovered. As the Spanish retreated across the causeways, they were intercepted by the Aztecs in canoes. Approximately 600 Spaniards were killed, many trying to escape with their gold and silver treasures from the Aztecs.

South of Mexico lay another great empire. The kingdom of the Incas stretched for 2,500 miles through the present-day countries of Ecuador, Peru and Chile. From the Incan capital at Cuzco, high in the Andes Mountains, their king, Atahualpa, directed an army of at least 50,000 troops. Against this powerful empire, the Spanish sent only a few hundred conquistadors. They were led by Francisco Pizarro, who had fought against the Moors in Spain and who later came to the New World. In 1513, he accompanied Vasco Nuñez de Balboa, the first European to reach the Pacific Ocean.

Pizarro was inspired by the success of Cortés. Hearing that the Incans possessed a rich treasure in gold and silver, Pizarro decided to take control of the Incan Empire. He used much the same strategy as Cortés had followed in Mexico. The Spanish possessed superior weapons—armor, steel swords, horses, and arquebuses. By contrast, the Incas had clubs with ends made of bronze, and stones hurled from slingshots. They were also divided by a civil war that had weakened the empire.

Pizarro made the most of his advantages. In November 1532, he entered the town of Cajamarca on the road to Cuzco with an army of fewer than 200 men. Before him lay Atahualpa with thousands of infantry. Atahualpa was so confident that he could defeat Pizarro that he agreed to come into the city with a small escort and meet with the conquistador. Meanwhile, Pizarro hid his infantry and their arquebuses in a building on the town square. As Atahualpa entered the town, the Spanish fired from their hiding places. Incas accompanying Atahualpa were immediately hit and killed. The rest of Pizarro's men, some on horseback, sprang from hiding and began to kill the rest of the Incas. In only 30 minutes, the Incas had been defeated and their king captured. Muskets and gunpowder had again proved to be decisive.

With Atahualpa in his control, Pizarro now believed he could run the empire. At first he tried to trick Atahualpa. Pizarro demanded a huge ransom of gold and silver for the king's release. But he never had any intention of releasing Atahualpa. Instead, he hoped to rule through him, just as Cortés had attempted to rule through Montezuma. But some of Pizarro's subordinates feared that with the king still alive, he might inspire a rebellion. Therefore, Pizarro finally ordered Atahualpa's execution in August 1533. After Atahualpa's death, Incan revolts broke out. With their superior weapons, however, the Spanish were successful in defeating the Indians and conquering their empire.

EUROPE VIES FOR CONTROL OF TRADE AND EMPIRE

While the Spanish were establishing a foothold in South America, other European nations were exploring the lands that lay northward. In 1608, French explorer Samuel de Champlain founded a colony on the Hudson River, naming it Montreal. He erected walls around the town with cannon to protect it and dug a moat outside the walls. In the following year, Champlain hoped to continue his explorations in North America. But the Indians he met told him that his way would be barred by the powerful Iroquois confederacy. This was a league of five Indian nations, whose capital was located in present-day New York State.

Champlain's Indian friends were impressed with the arqubuses he carried. They suggested that he and his soldiers join them in a raid against the Iroquois. The Iroquois league was hated by other Indians, such as the Ottawas, Hurons, and Algonquins, who had been defeated by the Iroquois in battle. Champlain agreed to join the Indians in an attack against the Iroquois that began in June 1609. Traveling southward from the Hudson River, Champlain and his allies encountered the Iroquois canoes at a place the Indians called Ticonderoga, in northern New York.

The Iroquois put into shore, and during the night, they built a wooded defense structure to protect themselves from a surprise attack. The next morning, Champlain and his men

After the French explorer Samuel de Champlain founded the colony of Montreal in 1608, he established alliances with native American tribes in the area to fight the powerful Iroquois. Here, a French soldier fires upon the enemy Iroquois with an arquebus, a weapon far more powerful than the Iroquois's arrows, while Indians allied with the French look on. As their chief falls, the other Iroquois flee.

donned their armor. Then they hid themselves in the canoes of their Indian allies as they were paddled toward the Iroquois positioned on shore. The Indian warriors advanced from the shore, and the Iroquois came out from their defenses to meet their enemy. Suddenly, Champlain and his men appeared and headed toward the Iroquois. "I looked at them," he later wrote, "and they looked at me. When I saw them getting ready to shoot their arrows at us, I leveled my arquebus, which I had loaded with four balls, and aimed straight at one of the three chiefs. The shot brought down two and wounded another. On this our Indians set up such a yelling that one would not have heard a thunderclap, and all the while the arrows flew thick on both sides. . . . As I was reloading, one of my companions fired a shot from the woods [at the Iroquois], which so increased their astonishment that, seeing their chiefs dead, they abandoned the field and fled into the depth of the forest."[42]

This encounter, involving guns and gunpowder, began an alliance between the French and the region's Indians that lasted for more than 150 years. It also turned the Iroquois into the enemies of the French colony in Canada. During the seventeenth century, they would take their revenge against the French. The Iroquois launched numerous raids against French settlements, killing men, women, and children. The Iroquois used hatchets, knives, and bows and arrows; they had also acquired arquebuses. The Indians traded furs for guns with Dutch merchants, who had established settlements at New Amsterdam (later called New York) and Albany along the Hudson River in northern New York. Indeed, the Iroquois became the allies of the Dutch and later the English, who captured New Amsterdam in 1664.

The struggle between the Dutch and English in the North America was part of a greater war for control of trade that was occurring in Europe. Holland built a large fleet during the seventeenth century. It included enormous, square-sailed ships that had to be large enough to carry cannon. Sailors now had to be trained to operate the cannon and hit enemy ships with their fire. With these ships, the Dutch tried to control trading routes to the East Indies, where they took over some of the colonies once controlled by the Portuguese. The Dutch ships also tried to dominate the trade routes to various ports in Western Europe.

The English vied with the Dutch for control of the sea trade, leading to a series of naval wars during the seventeenth century. Ships fought each other in long rows, called lines of battle. They would draw close to each other and then fire their cannons again and again, trying to disable enemy ships and kill enemy crews. In 1673, for example, the Dutch and English navies participated in three enormous battles in the North Sea near England. As many as 150 ships fought in these contests carrying almost 10,000 cannon.[43]

The long lines of battle on the sea were reflected in lines of infantry that now fought each other on land. Spanish, French, Swedish, and Austrian kings struggled to build European empires. In earlier years, European generals had created great squares of pikemen, sometimes 30 lines deep. On a battlefield, these strong squares could not easily be broken by cavalry charges. During the seventeenth century, however, pikemen were placed in the center, with arquebusiers, or musketeers, on the wings. Men were now placed in ranks six lines deep. The musketeers could shoot from the flanks and weaken the enemy, then the pikemen could charge. The thinner ranks could maneuver more easily across a battlefield. They were also longer and meant that more musketeers could fire at the enemy.

Muskets were also improved. In the seventeenth century, a new flintlock musket was introduced to replace the matchlock. A piece of flint was put in the hammer or lock instead of the match. When a musketeer pulled the trigger, the flint would descend and strike a steel latch, setting off sparks that would light the gunpowder in the pan of the musket. The flint was not as likely to be affected by rain and dampness as the match. As historian John Childs wrote, the flintlock was also "lighter [than the matchlock], could be fired from the shoulder [while the matchlock was held against the chest], was more accurate, and had double the rate of fire."[44]

In addition, paper cartridges were developed that contained a ball and powder. This also reduced the loading time because a musketeer did not have to measure out the powder and place it and the ball in the musket in separate steps. A musketeer bit off one end of a cartridge and poured some of the powder into the firing pan. Then he poured the rest of the powder into the muzzle of the gun, dropped in the ball, wadded up the paper from the cartridge and rammed it down to hold the ball in the musket. Next the soldier raised the hammer on the end of the gun, which also exposed the priming pan, and pulled the trigger. The flint would strike the metal latch and produce sparks, igniting the gunpowder.

That's if the soldier was lucky. The powder might also flash but not ignite. This was called "a flash in the pan."

A well-trained infantryman could fire three or four shots per minute. By the end of the century, the musket was also being equipped with a bayonet. This was similar to a long dagger that could be attached to the end of a musket. Once the infantryman had fired, he could then attach the bayonet and charge his enemy.

Muskets powered by gunpowder now became all-purpose weapons. Meanwhile cavalry had begun carrying pistols, which were also powered by gunpowder. To support cavalry and infantry, armies carried greater and greater numbers of cannon. In the past, these gunpowder-fired weapons had been used alongside crossbows and pikes. By the beginning of the eighteenth century, however, gunpowder weapons had come to dominate warfare.

5

The First Rifles and Muskets

During the eighteenth century, the great states of Europe built larger and larger armies. Long lines of infantry and cavalry engaged each other on the battlefield. Since every soldier was armed with a gun powered by gunpowder, the death toll in battle became much higher. There were also improvements in artillery, which became more accurate and could kill even more soldiers.

Meanwhile, in North America a new style of warfare emerged. Colonial settlers and their Indian allies used guerrilla warfare against their enemies. The colonists also developed a different type of firearm, the rifle, which was far more accurate than the musket.

While Europe depended on professional armies, in North America militias made up of citizen soldiers often fought on the battlefield. These soldiers, armed with their muskets and rifles, helped win the American Revolution. During the French Revolution, at the end of the eighteenth century, citizen soldiers were transformed into enormous professional armies.

GUNPOWDER ON THE BATTLEFIELD

Louis XIV (reigned 1643–1715) was known as the Sun King. His court at Versailles in France was considered the most brilliant in Europe because of its wealth and splendor. Louis dreamed of making France the greatest power on the continent. To accomplish this goal, he vastly increased the size of his armies. While an army in the past might number 10,000 to 20,000 men, Louis's army had risen to over 300,000 by 1700.[45]

A tapestry from Blenheim Palace in southern Germany shows English commander John Churchill preparing his troops for battle against French forces. English cavalry, supported by artillery, charged the French squadrons. The French suffered heavy casualties and were forced to retreat from the region.

Other states, like Great Britain and Austria, tried to prevent France from becoming more powerful and expanding its control into central Europe. As a result, they also had to build up their armies.

In 1704, the French armies commanded by Marshall Camille de Tallard fortified a position at Blenheim, a town in southern Germany. Here they were met by the British and Austrians commanded by John Churchill (who later became the Duke of Marlborough). Each side commanded an army of over 50,000 men. In addition to this army, Louis XIV had other forces operating throughout Europe. Marlborough knew there were grave risks. If he lost the battle, it might leave the French as the dominant power in Europe. Before the battle, Marlborough addressed his troops: "I know the danger," he said, "yet a battle is absolutely necessary, and I rely on the bravery and discipline of the troops. . . ."[46]

At first Marlborough tried to destroy the French forces in the town of Blenheim, located on one flank of the French position. But he was unsuccessful, and after a fierce struggle, the French forces held. Marlborough reformed his men and massed a giant cavalry force of 8,000 troops in the center of his line. Just after five o'clock in the afternoon, the cavalry began to advance, supported by artillery. They charged up a hill, where the French cavalry force awaited them. The French fired, and Marlborough's cavalry at first seemed stunned by the gunfire. "Marlborough instantly ordered a charge along the line. The . . . cavalry galloped forward at the enemy's squadrons, and the hearts of the French horsemen failed them. Discharging their carbines [small muskets] at an idle [long] distance, they wheeled round and spurred from the field, leaving the nine-infantry battalions of their comrades to be ridden down by the torrent of the allied cavalry. The battle was now won."[47] Casualties were heavy, with over 38,000 of the French killed or wounded. But it was a great victory, and Louis's armies were pushed back from central Europe.

The wars between France and other European states continued during the eighteenth century. Each country recruited professional armies, consisting of trained and disciplined soldiers. The troops had to be well disciplined to stand up against the frightening conditions on the battle-field. They were carefully drilled so that as one line finished firing, another line would step forward and fire at the enemy. Meanwhile the first line would reload, then the second, and so forth, as other lines fired. This enabled soldiers to fire continually at the enemy.

Muskets, however, were not effective at much beyond 50 to 80 yards. They were smoothbore weapons—that is, the inside of the barrels was smooth—and the bullets did not fit snugly inside the barrels. So lines of enemy troops had to stand at close quarters to do any damage. As historian Jeremy Black wrote: "The exchange of fire at close quarters . . . between lines of closely packed troops, the battlefield use of artillery firing . . . and cavalry engagements . . . all produced a large number of casualties."[48]

During the eighteenth century, artillery continuously improved, becoming more and more deadly. In France, for example, guns were equipped with better sights so gunners could aim more accurately. Cannon became lighter and were mounted on strong gun carriages with large wheels that transported them into battle quickly and efficiently. The gunners themselves were also better trained to operate their guns.

They used a variety of pieces. These included cannon powered by gunpowder that fired directly at an oncoming army. In addition, the gunners used howitzers and mortars that lofted shot high into the air. Solid balls were fired from cannon and exploding shot was used in howitzers. These could strike an enemy at several hundred yards. As the enemy drew closer, gunners used canister shot—a package of balls contained in a can that broke apart as it was fired. If they were closely packed together in a line, the canister shot could hit a great number of soldiers.

Describing the experience of battle, an officer wrote that "the balls flew about like hail." He added, "I admire and adore that kind of Providence who hath been my protector and preserver of my life and limbs during such a cannonading of nine hours as could not possibly be exceeded . . . there were batteries [of cannon] continually playing upon our front and both flanks."[49]

Cavalry charges, like the one at Blenheim, were also brutal. Horsemen used a combination of gunfire from carbines (short muskets) and pistols as well as slashing sabers. Describing a battle against the French, one British officer recalled, "They rode up to us with pistol in each hand, and their broad swords slung on their wrists. As soon as they had fired their pistols they flung them at our heads, clapped spurs and rode upon us sword in hand." [50] Although the British were initially pushed back, they rallied and defeated the French.

Gunpowder-fired weapons made warfare in the eighteenth century far more brutal with casualties much higher than in earlier times. Unfortunately, the revolution in firepower was not accompanied by improvements in medicine, and many soldiers who were injured on the battlefield died of their wounds.

GUNPOWDER IN NORTH AMERICA

The wars between France and England in Europe were also fought out in North America. The French had established an empire in Canada. From Quebec and Montreal on the Hudson River, they carried on a fur trade with the Indians who lived in the interior. During the eighteenth century, they also established a line of forts along the Ohio River valley. The French, together with their Indian allies, wanted to enclose the English colonies that had sprung up along the Atlantic Coast and prevent them from expanding inland. Since the French population in Canada was only about 100,000, they needed the help of the Indian warriors with whom they traded. By contrast, the British colonists had reached a population of 1.5 million by the middle of the eighteenth century.

To defend themselves against the French and their allies, the English colonists relied on the militia system. Every male from age 16 to 60 was expected to serve in the militia. The standard weapon for the militia was the flintlock musket, also called the Brown Bess. Militiamen were expected to keep their muskets working properly, and train together regularly so they would be ready to defend their settlements in case of attack. Of course, they were not the only ones armed with muskets.

The Indian allies of the French carried muskets, as did the Iroquois Indians who were allied to the English. As historians Allan Millet and Peter Maslowski wrote, the Indians, "at least in New England . . . learned how to cast bullets, replace worn flints, . . . and make a variety of other repairs. Only one technical capability continued to elude Indians. They never mastered gunpowder production and experienced numerous powder shortages."[51]

While the Indians may have needed to rely on the French or English for supplies of gunpowder, they had developed a method of fighting that was far superior to that practiced by the colonials. The Indians knew how to take advantage of the wooded terrain of North America. They were masters of guerrilla fighting—setting ambushes, shooting from behind trees, and waiting until their enemy was reloading to charge and kill him with a knife or tomahawk.

The English colonists were slow to adopt the Indian style of warfare. Instead, they wanted to use the same type of warfare practiced in Europe. This meant marching packed together in columns and fighting in lines. As Millet and Maslowski wrote, "Despite blundering into ambush after ambush, colonists persisted in marching in close order, so that, as one Indian said, 'it was as easy to hit them as to hit [a] house.' The colonists' reluctance to adjust to New World conditions was partly psychological. They considered Indian warfare barbaric; if Europeans fought in the same way, would they not also be barbarians?"[52]

But at least some of the English colonists gradually began to adopt the Indian style of warfare. The French also joined their Indian allies in raids and ambushes against English settlements. In 1754, war broke out in North America between the English and the French. Called the French and Indian War, it would be known as the Seven Years' War in Europe. In the opening battle

During the French and Indian War, British troops under General Edward Braddock suffered a disastrous defeat at the hands of the French and their Native-American allies. Protected by rocks and trees, the Indians fired their muskets at the British soldiers who were commanded to "stand and fight like men, not hide like cowards."

of the French and Indian War a 21-year-old Virginia surveyor named George Washington led a group of colonials in a surprise attack on a small French force in the Ohio Valley. They made a night march against the French in their camp. "As black as pitch," Washington later wrote. "The path was hardly wide enough for one man, we often lost it and could not find it again for 15 or 20 minutes and we often tumbled over each other in the dark." [53] Early the next morning they attacked from the woods and surprised the French who were still at their camp. With their muskets, Washington and his men killed nine of the French and took 21 prisoners. Washington was well aware of the value of Indian-style warfare.

This lesson was lost on the English regular troops. In 1755, the English appointed General Edward Braddock to carry on the war against the French. Braddock outfitted an army of approximately 2,000 men to march against the French stronghold at Fort Duquesne in the Ohio Valley. In June, Braddock headed west with a force of British regulars, cannon, and a few Virginia militia. At the head of the column were some 300 axemen, hired to cut a road to Fort Duquesne.

Braddock was aware that his army might be ambushed along the way, so he sent out men on the flanks and into the woods to scout for the enemy. But the flankers somehow missed the French and their Indian allies. On July 9, 1755, the French set up an ambush a few miles from Fort Duquesne and annihilated the English army.

The French and Indian War turned out to be a mixture of European and colonial style warfare. There were bloody ambushes as well as successful sieges. By 1759, the English had succeeded in capturing most of the important French strongholds and were laying siege to Quebec on the Hudson River. With an army of almost 10,000 troops, English general James Wolfe began the siege in June. Opposing him were the French forces commanded by Marquis Louis Joseph de Montcalm. General Montcalm had built strong defenses around the city and had more than 100 guns mounted on its ramparts. Wolfe had to move against these defenses fairly quickly because the St. Lawrence River would begin to freeze in the fall, forcing his ships and soldiers to leave for home.

Eventually, Wolfe succeeded in ascending steep cliffs along a trail west of the city. On September 13, he assembled almost

5,000 of his troops on the Plains of Abraham. Montcalm brought an equal number of soldiers out of the city. It was the first and only European style battle of the French and Indian War. The English advanced to within 40 yards of the French, firing their muskets again and again. The enemy's front collapsed. Wolfe was killed in the battle, and Montcalm lost his life during the retreat of his army into Quebec. But the city fell. Montreal was taken in 1760, and the French Empire in North America became English.

Braddock's Defeat

General Braddock had been given the task of building a road to Fort Duquesne, then defeating the French army there. From the beginning, Braddock realized that it was a difficult undertaking. "Nothing can well be worse than the road I have already passed and I have an hundred and ten miles to march through an uninhabited wilderness over steep rock mountains and almost impassable morasses."* To speed the task, Braddock decided to leave some of his supplies behind and push on with a smaller force to build the road. They made incredible progress, bringing them eight miles from Fort Duquesne. Meanwhile the French could not decide how to stop the British, whose forces far outnumbered theirs. However, the French did have 800 Indian allies at the fort. Finally, the French commander, Sieur De Contrecoeur, decided to send them out with a few of his soldiers. They were led by Captain Daniel Beaujeu, who planned to ambush the enemy. As the English moved forward, they saw the French advancing. The English fired, killing Beaujeu. But the Indians dispersed into the woods. From the cover of the trees, they began to fire on the British troops who were standing on the road. The Virginia militia took cover and some of the British regulars tried to do the same. But Braddock commanded them to stand up and fight like men, not hide like cowards. Nothing could have been worse. They were picked off in masses by the Indians firing their muskets from behind the trees. Finally, Braddock himself was fatally wounded. The English were forced to retreat, having lost most of their troops.

*Brian Connell, *The Savage Years* (New York: Harper Brothers, 1959), pp. 54–55.

Winning the French and Indian War was very expensive for the English government. To pay off some of these expenses, the English Parliament decided to tax the American colonies during the 1760s. The colonists resisted, saying that they had never been consulted about these taxes and were not represented in Parliament. The disagreement between England and its colonies led directly to the outbreak of the American Revolution in 1775.

The first battles at Lexington and Concord, Massachusetts, occurred as the British troops tried to take control of the colonists' gunpowder. (See Chapter One.) After these battles, the British retreated into Boston where they were blockaded by a force of colonial militia. Unlike the professional British army, the colonials formed a citizen army, among the first of its kind.

In June 1775, this citizen army tried to tighten the blockade against the British by fortifying a position on Breed's Hill that looked down on the city of Boston. The British retaliated by storming the hill. In a fierce struggle known as the Battle of Bunker Hill, on June 17, the militia withstood charge after charge by British regulars. The colonials were finally forced to retreat when they ran out of gunpowder. Nevertheless, they had defended themselves against the mighty British army, which suffered almost three times as many casualties as the colonials.

Following the battle, George Washington took command of the army around Boston. Washington and the Continental Congress, which was in charge of directing the American fight for independence, realized that a militia alone was not sufficient to win a war. Militiamen were used to fighting only in their geographic region. Washington realized that he would need an army that could move up and down the Atlantic seaboard to defend it wherever the English tried to take control.

Congress, therefore, authorized the formation of the Continental Army. This would be a force of trained regulars

John Trumbull's famous painting depicts the Battle of Bunker Hill. During the fierce battle, American militiamen withstood charge after charge by the British. They eventually ran out of gunpowder and were forced to retreat.

drawn from various regions of North America. They did not replace the militia. The Continentals were expected to form the heart of the army, with the militia serving as supporting troops. But even these Continentals were different from European professional soldiers. Although they wore uniforms, "they asserted their personal independence by wearing jaunty hats and long hair despite . . . their officers' insistence upon conformity in dress and appearance. Furthermore, they were only temporary regulars. Unlike European professionals, they understood the war's goals and would fight until they were achieved, but then they intended to return to civilian life."[55]

During the blockade of Boston, troops began arriving from Virginia and Maryland to form the new Continental Army. Some of the soldiers brought with them a weapon known as a rifle. The term *rifling* means to put grooves inside the barrel of a gun. This enables the bullet to rotate when it is fired, improving its accuracy. Although invented in Europe several centuries earlier, rifling was first practiced on the American frontier. Rifles were thinner and slightly longer than muskets. They fired smaller bullets, so frontiersmen could use less lead and powder, saving money. The rifle was also deadlier than a musket at long distances. A frontiersman could hit a target at 250 yards, versus 50 yards with a musket. However, the rifle took longer to load. A frontiersman had to place the bullet in a piece of greased buckskin to give it a tighter fit inside the rifle. Then he would push the bullet down the barrel with a ramrod.[56]

During the Revolutionary War, the combination of militia and Continentals together with rifles and muskets proved very effective in the Americans' most important victories. In the summer of 1777, for example, British General John Burgoyne led a large army southward from Canada to capture Albany, New York, on the Hudson River. On its march southward, Burgoyne's army met a force of American Continentals and militia near Saratoga, just north of Albany. Under the command of General Horatio Gates, this citizen army defeated the British—considered the greatest professional army in the world. American soldiers drove back the British with volley after volley of musket fire. Trained sharpshooters, armed with rifles, also took a toll on the English commanders. As Burgoyne himself later wrote: "The enemy had with their army great numbers of marksmen, armed with rifle-barrel pieces. . . . In this action, many placed themselves in high trees in the rear of their own line, and there was seldom a minute's interval of smoke in any part of our line without officers being taken off by single shots."[57] One of these shots hit General Simon Fraser, the British army's second in command, leading to a general retreat and eventual surrender.

American rifles, muskets, and gunpowder had been decisive. The American victory at Saratoga was the turning point of the Revolutionary War. It brought France into the war against England, providing military support that would eventually lead to British defeat.

The foundation for this final defeat was laid during the southern campaign of 1781. Before the campaign began, the British had successfully occupied the major cities of Charleston, South Carolina, and Savannah, Georgia, on the coast. They had also built a line of smaller posts in the interior. But these were difficult to defend because of American guerrilla forces. The Revolutionary War was among the first conflicts in which guerrilla forces participated.

The guerrillas, often armed with rifles, were led by commanders like Francis Marion. Born in South Carolina about 1732, Marion joined the American army at the outbreak of the revolution. He later he formed a guerrilla force which struck British supply posts then melted away without being caught. Marion was known as the "Swamp Fox" for his ability to hide his men in the Carolina swamps so British troops could not find them.

Against the American guerrillas, English loyalists formed military bands of their own. In the Carolinas there were many Scots and Irish immigrants with strong loyalties to the English king. Known as Tories, they formed military units under leaders such as Major Patrick Ferguson. A 36-year-old Scotsman, Ferguson had invented a rifle that would have revolutionized warfare. Instead of loading from the muzzle, it was loaded from the other end, or breech. It could fire faster than a musket and

British General John Burgoyne surrenders to the American Continentals at the town of Saratoga. As well-trained American sharpshooters picked off some of the British officers, the demoralized British troops were soon forced to surrender.

could hit a target at 500 yards. But Ferguson was too far ahead of his time, and the rifle was not adopted.

Such a rifle might have been very useful to Ferguson and his men when they were cornered by an American force of militia at Kings Mountain, South Carolina, on October 7, 1780. American riflemen overpowered Ferguson and his troops. Ferguson was killed when he was shot out of the saddle of his horse by a marksman. His entire force was destroyed.

American victories undermined the British position in the Carolinas and Georgia. Eventually, the English army, commanded by General Charles Cornwallis, abandoned the Carolinas to seek safety in Virginia. Here Cornwallis was eventually besieged by American and French forces at Yorktown. He surrendered on October 19, 1781. America had won its independence.

The American citizen army that had won the Revolutionary War became a model for another army a decade later. In 1789, a revolution in France overthrew the corrupt monarchy of Louis XVI. Under the monarchy, French armies had been commanded by the nobility. Many of the nobles, however, were executed during the revolution. In their place, new leaders emerged. The French revolutionary government also ordered all able-bodied men between the ages of 18 and 25 to serve in the army. As a result, France created enormous citizen armies. Nothing this large had ever been seen before in Europe. These armies successfully defended French territory against other European

Battle of Cowpens

Less than three months after the battle of King's Mountain, a small American army won another victory that was just as stunning. Under the command of General Daniel Morgan, a combined force of Continentals and militia defeated a British army led by Colonel Banastre Tarleton. Colonel Tarleton had won a reputation for his brutality in attacking civilians. He also butchered enemy troops after they had surrendered. Morgan had figured out how to use his riflemen, militia, and Continentals to the best advantage against Tarleton. At the Battle of Cowpens on January 17, 1781, Morgan hid his riflemen in trees. From this position, they shot down many of Tarleton's cavalry as they approached the battle site. Behind the riflemen, Morgan had placed a line of militia. As the British charged, he told the militia to fire only two volleys and then retreat. He knew that militia were often frightened off by English bayonet charges and could only be counted on to take a minor part in a battle. The militia did their job, killing as many British regulars as they could. Then they retreated. As the British kept advancing, they were met by volley after volley from Morgan's Continentals. The result was a total victory in which almost the entire British force was killed or captured. Only Tarleton and a few of his men escaped.

states that wanted to put an end to the French Revolution. They regarded it as a threat to their own monarchies.

Gradually, the French followed up their victories by advancing against neighboring states. Under the command of General Napoleon Bonaparte, the French used gunpowder to wage total war in Europe. Gunpowder and enormous professional armies now changed the face of warfare forever.

6

The Weapons Revolution

AT ISSUE

In 1805, French emperor Napoleon won a decisive victory over the Russians and Austrians at the Battle of Austerlitz in central Europe. The battlefield was covered with the smoke of gunpowder as thousands of soldiers fought each other in bloody combat. More than 150,000 troops were engaged at Austerlitz, and the casualties were enormous. The Russians and Austrians lost almost 25 percent of their troops.

The battle was fought with smoothbore muzzleloading muskets. But as the nineteenth century continued, the face of warfare changed. Gunpowder was now combined with more deadly weapons. These included muzzleloaders with percussion systems, muzzleloaders with rifled barrels and bullets that could kill at longer distances, and finally breechloaders.

Meanwhile, gunpowder was also being used for other purposes. In the United States, E.I. DuPont invented a more powerful type of gunpowder that was blasting out mines and carving out roadbeds for railroads. DuPont and other powder manufacturers were involved in a booming business.

THE NAPOLEONIC WARS

The Napoleonic Wars, which began in the late eighteenth century and continued until 1815, pitted France against the other powers of Europe. At first, Napoleon was successful in defeating his enemies, extending the French Empire over huge territories in central Europe. Napoleon had risen through the

Emperor Napoleon's enormous armies extended the boundaries of the French Empire into central Europe. In 1815, a grand alliance of European countries finally defeated Napoleon at the Battle of Waterloo, portrayed in this painting. The opposing armies are enveloped by the smoke of smoothbore muzzleloading muskets and cannon-fire.

ranks as an artillery expert. In his battles, he often massed large numbers of cannon that blew huge holes in the lines of opposing armies. This method had worked well for the French at the Battle of Austerlitz. Napoleon also put enormous armies in the field. In 1812, for example, he led a force of more than

600,000 men into Russia. Most of these soldiers either died in battle or lost their lives during the cold, snowy Russian winter. Much weakened, Napoleon found himself facing a grand alliance of European nations, including England, Austria, Prussia, and Russia. They opposed him with an army even larger than one that he could recruit. Eventually, Napoleon was defeated at the Battle of Waterloo in 1815. Approximately 200,000 men participated in the battle, with casualties reaching almost 50,000.

Gunpowder-fired weapons began to account for greater and greater numbers of deaths on the battlefield. As historian David Gates pointed out, "the Napoleonic War claimed the lives of 38 percent of the young men born in France from 1790 to 1795." [58] Indeed, it was known as the Great War, because no other conflict up to that time had led to so many casualties.

Star-Spangled Banner

While the English were fighting Napoleon, they were also engaged in a conflict with the United States, called the War of 1812. As the war began, U.S. and English forces battled in the west around Detroit. Battles also took place in western New York on the Niagara River and Lake Erie. In 1814, British forces invaded Washington, D.C., and burned the Capitol and the White House. A British force then sailed up the Chesapeake Bay toward Baltimore. In September, the British bombarded Fort McHenry, guarding the approach to Baltimore. During the bombardment, they used Congreve rockets. These were wooden tubes loaded with gunpowder that carried large iron tips on the ends. They were fired from rocket launchers. As the rockets flew into the night over Fort McHenry, they left long trails of fire behind them. The British also fired explosive shells from their cannon. Watching the bombardment was a lawyer named Francis Scott Key. Afterward, he wrote the words for the Star-Spangled Banner, which became the national anthem of the United States. Inspired by the bombardment, Key included the lines, ". . . the rocket's red glare, the bombs bursting in air, gave proof through the night that our flag was still there" in the anthem.

In this painting, a young lawyer named Francis Scott Key watches the bombardment of Fort McHenry during the War of 1812. British-launched Congreve rockets have miraculously missed the American flag. Awed by the "rocket's red glare," Key later wrote the "Star-Spangled Banner," which became the American national anthem.

ALEXANDER FORSYTH'S PERCUSSION SYSTEM

Following the allied victory at Waterloo, Europe enjoyed a century without a major war on the continent. However, advances in the development of weapons using gunpowder continued. In England, Reverend Alexander Forsyth invented a new method of firing muzzleloading weapons. Reverend Forsyth enjoyed hunting. However, when he fired his gun using a flintlock mechanism, he discovered that the ducks sometimes saw the sparks and dived under water before he could discharge his bullet and hit them.

During the early nineteenth century, Forsyth developed a percussion system for firing weapons that replaced the flintlock mechanism. The percussion system included a cap that could be made out of paper or metal. The cap contained an explosive substance called fulminate. The fulminate was often mercury, although other substances were also used. As a hunter or soldier pulled the trigger on his musket, a thin piece of metal shaped like a needle descended and pierced the cap on the breech of the gun. The fulminate exploded and ignited the gunpowder in the musket, firing the bullet. Weapons with percussion caps could be fired faster than muskets using the old flintlock system. The metal caps also avoided the problem of rain or moisture preventing the sparks from the flintlock igniting gunpowder in a musket. Many older muskets were converted to percussion-firing weapons, and new muskets were manufactured with the percussion caps.

SAMUEL COLT'S REVOLVERS

Meanwhile, in the United States inventors were also experimenting with new types of weapons that would use gunpowder. Among them was Samuel Colt. Born in Hartford, Connecticut, in 1814, Colt studied existing guns, trying to develop one that would shoot more than one shot without reloading. As historian Geoffrey Perrett wrote: "The solution came to Colt while he was still in his teens, during a year spent as a seaman, watching the spokes of a helmsman's wheel coming successively into line with a clutch. The clutch could be set to stop the wheel at any spoke. Colt whittled a model revolver from wood and, back on shore, tried to make one from metal."[59] Eventually he invented a working revolver in 1835. The early Colt revolver had several chambers and was loaded with a rammer—a miniature ramrod—through the muzzle. The cartridges were made of linen or paper, containing gunpowder and a bullet. These revolvers were fired using a percussion cap.

At first, Colt's revolvers were not widely used. Soldiers were accustomed to the old style muskets. On the frontier, however, the army began to discover that the revolvers gave them a distinct advantage in fighting Indians. The Indians did not realize that after firing one shot, the soldiers could so easily fire again. When the mounted warriors charged on their horses, they met a volley of gunfire from the army. As a result, the revolver began to be more widely accepted among the soldiers.

In 1845, Mexico and the United States went to war over control of disputed territories in the Southwest and California. President James Polk and other political leaders believed that it was part of the Manifest Destiny of the United States to control the entire North American continent. Colt's revolver was used by United States infantry during the war. U.S. troops also proved that they were masters of artillery. An artillery school had been established to train expert gunners. They demonstrated their value in battle after battle during the Mexican War where they out-dueled the Mexican artillery. The U.S. gunners played a decisive role in the final battles of the war that led to the fall of Mexico City, the capital of Mexico, in 1847. As a result of the war, the United States acquired 530,000 square miles from Mexico, which included the territories that are now New Mexico and California.

SUPPLIERS OF GUNPOWDER

The gunpowder with which the United States Army fought the war in Mexico was provided by a variety of American firms. The largest supplier was a manufacturer named E.I. DuPont, located near Wilmington, Delaware. The company had been founded by Eleuthere Irenee DuPont, who had learned the science of gunpowder making in France. Immigrating to the United States in 1800, he found the quality of the local gunpowder inferior to what he had seen in Europe. DuPont purchased a large 95 acre farm on the Brandywine River in Delaware for about $6,700. The land had waterpower to run mills, as well as extensive woodlands for charcoal—a major ingredient in gunpowder. Construction of the mills began in 1802, and the firm continued to expand over the next decades.

Gunpowder was used not only for military weapons, but also in guns for hunting and in mining. Gunpowder was used to blast openings in large rock formations where mines could be developed. Coal and iron were being mined in states such as Pennsylvania. Coal was used as a fuel, while iron was manufactured into machinery for factories and into engines that were powering new railroads. In 1857, Lammot Du Pont, Irenee's grandson, developed a more effective powder for mining. Called "B" powder, it used sodium nitrate from Chile and Peru instead of potassium nitrate, which came mainly from India.

MINIE RIFLES AND THE NEEDLE GUN

While the demand for gunpowder in mining continued to grow, its primary use was still military weapons. These continued to become more powerful, due to inventions in Europe and the United States. One of these was the minie ball, invented in 1849 by Captain Claude-Etienne Minie of the French army. European soldiers began using the minie ball in their rifled muskets during the 1850s. In the past, rifles had been difficult to load. However, the minie ball, which was shaped like a cone, solved this problem. The minie ball had grooves and an expanding base. A soldier loaded a cartridge containing powder and the minie into the muzzle of his musket. As the powder was ignited by a percussion cap, the base of the minie would expand, gripping the grooves of a rifled barrel. The minie rifle enabled soldiers to load faster and fire 10 times farther than the old smoothbore musket, with the same accuracy.

The new minie rifles were carried by French and British soldiers during the Crimean War (1853–1856). This conflict broke out when Russian troops invaded part of the Turkish Empire. In retaliation, France and Britain helped defend the Turks and sent troops to the Russian territory of Crimea— a peninsula in the Black Sea. Russian troops were still using old smoothbore muskets. When the Russians tried to charge, they were picked off by the longer-range minie rifles before they could get near enough to hit the French and English soldiers.

The minie rifles were muzzleloaders. At the same time that the minie rifles were being used in Crimea, the Prussian Army in central Europe was adopting a new breechloading rifle. This is a rifle that can be loaded from the back instead of the front. Called the needle gun, this rifle was developed by Johann Nikolaus Von Dreyse during the 1840s. As a soldier pulled the trigger, a needle would be driven forward and penetrate the cartridge, igniting the powder and discharging the bullet. The breechloader enabled a soldier to load a rifle while he was lying down instead of standing up using a ramrod. The king of Prussia referred to the new gun as "a special dispensation of Providence for the strengthening of our National resources," adding that he wanted it to "be kept secret until the great part it is destined to play in history may couple it with the glory of Prussian arms in the extension of Europe." [60]

But the new weapon did not remain a secret, and other

nations soon adopted it for their armies, too. In addition, metal cartridges gradually replaced soft cartridges. The gunpowder and the bullet were contained in a small, sealed metal case. This enabled Colt to develop a breechloading revolver. It could be loaded in the rear with several metal cartridges and no longer needed a small ramrod, which had been used in the muzzleloading revolver.

THE CIVIL WAR

All the weapons developed over the past century were put to use during the most devastating conflict in American history—the Civil War. When the war began in 1861, the majority of the soldiers in the Federal and Confederate armies carried smoothbore muskets. In the South, mercury for percussion caps as well as gunpowder were at a premium. The Confederacy had very little manufacturing and depended for income mainly on selling its cotton. The Confederate government, therefore, asked Southerners to send in their thermometers that contained mercury. The mercury could be used in percussion caps. The Confederacy had only two gunpowder manufacturing operations. These were located in South Carolina and near Nashville, Tennessee. Eventually, the South established another manufacturing plant at Augusta, Georgia. The Confederacy obtained saltpeter from limestone caves, located in Tennessee, Alabama, Georgia, and Arkansas.

While the North had built hundreds of gunpowder plants, saltpeter was in short supply. Indeed, Lammot Du Pont went to England as the war began to purchase a large amount of saltpeter for the manufacture of gunpowder. (Gunpowder B was effective for blasting in mines but not in guns.) Many of the rifles used by Northern troops were manufactured at an arsenal in Springfield, Massachusetts. More than 840,000 Springfield rifles were produced between 1858 and 1865, when the Civil War ended.[61] They were rifled muzzleloading muskets using percussion ignition systems. Civil War soldiers used Burton bullets in their rifles, a variation of the minie bullet, as well as paper cartridges with 60 grains of gunpowder. In addition, rifled muskets, called Enfields, were imported from Great Britain.

With the minie system, the rifled muskets could produce a high number of casualties in any battle, especially against troops marching in closely packed lines across a battlefield. In September 1862, Confederate General Robert E. Lee led his Army of Northern Virginia in an invasion of Maryland. The Confederate invasion was stopped by a Union army commanded by General George B. McClellan at the Battle of Antietam on September 17, 1862. In a single day of fighting, more than 23,000 men were killed or wounded. It was the bloodiest day in American military history.

Lee retreated into Virginia. A few months later, his troops stopped an attack by Federal forces at Fredericksburg. The Union soldiers charged up a hill against the Confederates, who were standing behind defensive works. There, on December 13, 1862, more than 12,000 Union troops were killed or wounded. After getting a report of the disaster, President Abraham Lincoln remarked, "If there is a worse place than Hell, I am in it."[62]

As the war continued, weapons became more sophisticated and the number of soldiers killed grew even higher. Some soldiers were armed with breechloading rifles manufactured by the Sharps Rifle Manufacturing Company of Hartford, Connecticut. These rifles fired much faster than the muzzleloaders—about 10 rounds per minute. They were often carried by Sharpshooters, who were used as skirmishers out in front of the main lines to slow down opposing troops. Sharpshooters could also take positions in trees and other camouflaged locations and pick off enemy soldiers.

In 1863, General Lee again invaded the north. During the three-day battle of Gettysburg (July 1–3, 1863), Federal cavalry used Sharps rifles against Confederate cavalrymen who were still using muzzleloading rifles. On the final day of the battle, Lee made a frontal charge against the Union forces. Led by General George Pickett, the attack was known as Pickett's Charge. As the thin lines of Confederate troops moved slowly forward across the battlefield, they were decimated by Union cannon and infantry fire. Rifled muskets as well as rifled artillery were successful in destroying the charge

Gunpowder and the *Monitor*

Early in 1862, the U.S. government launched the *Monitor*, an ironclad ship with low flat decks and a turret in the center. The *Monitor* was described as a "cheesebox on a raft." But inside the cheesebox were two 16,000 pound smoothbore muzzleloading cannon. The cannon were placed on railroad tracks, so they could roll backward after firing. The guns produced an enormous recoil. The turret revolved, giving the cannon much wider range than earlier naval weapons.

On March 9, 1862, the *Monitor* met a Confederate ironclad, the *Merrimack*, at Hampton Roads, Virginia. The *Merrimack* had been attacking Federal ships made of wood and sinking them, jeopardizing Union control of Chesapeake Bay. The battle between the *Monitor* and *Merrimack* was the first engagement of ironclads in the history of naval warfare. The two ships fought for four hours. But neither could defeat the other. However, if the *Monitor* had used more gunpowder, it might have been able to achieve a victory. The guns were loaded with only one charge of powder each time they fired. But "these cannons could have handled three charges, and historians have speculated that, had they done so, the *Monitor* would have severely damaged or even sunk the Confederate vessel."* As it was, both ships disengaged and the *Merrimack* retreated, leaving the Union navy in command of the Chesapeake. A short time later, the *Merrimack* was destroyed when Union forces captured the harbor where it was anchored at Norfolk, Virginia.

*Wendy Wittman Clarke, "Pieces of History." *Smithsonian*, Nov. 2002, 66.

before it could ever penetrate the Union lines. Picket lost 50 percent of his troops.

During the remainder of the Civil War, more advanced weapons found their way into the hands of some of the troops. Union cavalry used Colt repeating rifles that could fire a number of shots without reloading. In 1864, General Ulysses Grant led the Federal armies southward into Virginia in a final series of campaigns to take the Confederate capital

Used by the Union Navy during the Civil War, the USS *Monitor* was an ironclad ship with low, flat decks and a turret that held two 16,000-pound smoothbore muzzleloading cannon. The turret revolved, giving the cannon a wide range. Because of the tremendous recoil, the cannon sat on tracks that allowed them to roll backward after they were fired.

One of the bloodiest battles of the Civil War was fought at Gettysburg, Pennsylvania. Federal cavalrymen were armed with the newly developed Sharps rifle, which fired 10 rounds per minute and were much deadlier than the muzzleloading rifles used by most of the Confederates.

at Richmond. The combined forces of Grant and Lee numbered over 200,000. The casualties were enormous. Finally, Grant approached the city of Petersburg, Virginia, which guarded Richmond. Lee entrenched his troops. This was the only way to give them some protection against the powerful gunpowder-fired weapons that were being used in the war.

However, Lee's forces were eventually overwhelmed and he surrendered on April 9, 1865. The Civil War was over. More than one million men had been killed or wounded among the Union and Confederate forces. Of these, 620,000 had died. This was a higher total than the combined number of Americans killed in World War I, World War II, and the Korean conflict.[64] Gunpowder, combined with sophisticated weapons, had created a new brand of murderous warfare.

7

Beyond Gunpowder

AT ISSUE

For several centuries, the muzzleloading musket powered by black gunpowder was the standard weapon on the battlefield. During the nineteenth century, however, a technological revolution transformed much of the world. Large factories were being built, new forms of transportation such as the railroad were developed, and faster methods of communication, like the telegraph and telephone, were invented.

Technology transformed weapons, as well. In a few decades, the muzzleloader was replaced by breechloaders, then repeating weapons. Artillery became far more powerful. Finally, black gunpowder itself was replaced by smokeless gunpowder.

All of these advances in weaponry were used in two terrible world wars that resulted in millions of casualties during the twentieth century. At the end of the Second World War, an even more lethal force than gunpowder—atomic power—appeared on the battlefield.

AUTOMATIC GUNS

Richard J. Gatling was born in North Carolina in 1818. As a young man he developed a machine to sow rice in fields and later opened a factory to produce other farm equipment. During the 1860s, Gatling invented a new rapid-fire gun. It consisted of six barrels, operated by a crank that revolved around and fired bullets. At first it fired paper cartridges, but these were soon replaced by metal cartridges. Following the Civil War, the

Taken at Fort McKeen in 1885, this photograph shows the six-barrel, rapid-fire Gatling gun. The gun was operated by a crank and fired metal cartridges. It was purchased by the U.S. Army to fight Native American Indians on the western frontier.

Gatling gun was purchased by the U.S. Army and used on the frontier in wars against the Native American Indians. By constantly improving the weapon, Gatling eventually developed a gun that shot 1,200 bullets per minute.

Meanwhile, another American inventor named Hiram Maxim was working on a different type of automatic weapon that would eventually replace the Gatling gun. Born in Maine in 1840, Maxim was fascinated by science. He eventually invented an electric light bulb that was the forerunner of the bulbs developed by Thomas Edison. But his main interest became the development of a rapid-fire gun, because it was something that many armies were interested in using. As a friend told him, "Hang your electricity and chemistry! If you want to make a pile of money, invent something that will enable these Europeans to cut each others' throats with greater facility."[65] During the 1880s, Maxim eventually invented an automatic machine gun. Instead of the crank, a soldier simply pressed the trigger to fire round after round of bullets.

The Gatling gun and Maxim's machine gun were used during the imperial wars of the nineteenth and twentieth centuries. Imperialism refers to the efforts by western powers, such as Great Britain, France, and Germany, to create empires. Much of the empire building occurred in Africa where European nations took control of vast territories. These became sources of raw materials, such as rubber, which was used in European factories to manufacture tires. Africa also served as a huge market for Europeans to sell manufactured goods, such as clothing. The Europeans used the Gatling gun against native armies that did not possess such a sophisticated weapon.

During the late nineteenth century, the United States also became an imperialist power. In the Spanish-American War, which broke out in 1898, U.S. forces wrested control of Puerto Rico and the Philippines from Spain. American troops also drove the Spanish out of Cuba and granted Cuba its independence. During the battle for Cuba, American forces successfully attacked San Juan Hill, which guarded the Spanish city of Santiago. It was a battery of three Gatling guns that helped clear the Spanish from San Juan Hill, resulting in an American victory.[66]

ADVANCEMENTS IN EXPLOSIVE POWDERS

When first invented, the Gatling gun used black gunpowder. In 1885, however, a French physics professor named Paul Vieille invented a replacement for gunpowder known as *poudre* B. It

This photograph, taken in Cuba, shows one of the three Gatling guns that helped U.S. forces capture San Juan Hill during the Spanish–American War. American troops defeated the Spanish, and Cuba became an independent nation.

consisted of nitrocellulose. This is a substance like cotton, treated with nitric and sulfuric acids. It was called guncotton. Nitrocellulose by itself is very volatile and hard to control. Vieille mixed the so-called guncotton with a gelatin and ether-alcohol to stabilize it. It could then be cut into flakes or grains and used as a propellant.

This new powder had several advantages over the old black gunpowder. First, it was more powerful. A soldier could now hit a target approximately 1,000 yards away. Second, the powder was smokeless. A smokeless powder meant that soldiers would not be seen when they fired their weapons. They could be hidden and were less likely to be attacked. After being fired, some black powder usually remained behind inside a gun barrel and eventually clogged it so the barrel had to be cleaned. Smokeless powder did not have this disadvantage. Finally, clouds of white smoke would not cover a battlefield, making it easier to direct an army of troops.

In 1887, Swiss chemist Alfred Nobel developed a smokeless gunpowder called cordite. Nobel also experimented with a substance called nitroglycerine. This was a very volatile substance that would explode if someone accidentally bumped against it. In 1886, however, Nobel had discovered that if nitroglycerine were combined with a substance like wood pulp, it was far less volatile. He called his new invention dynamite. It was far more powerful than black gunpowder. Dynamite replaced gunpowder in mining. Nitroglycerine was also combined with nitrocellulose to make smokeless powder.

Another substance, called TNT (trinitrotoluene), was discovered in 1905. It was also more powerful than gunpowder. TNT began to be used in mining. It was also packed into metal artillery shells as an explosive. TNT could produce far more damage and cause many more casualties than gunpowder on the battlefield. By the early twentieth century, armies were using smokeless powders as a propellant in small weapons such as rifles, pistols, and machine guns. The artillery relied on TNT as an explosive. TNT could also be mixed with other substances for this purpose.

These powerful shells were being used in large steel artillery pieces. Steel was much stronger than iron, which had been used in the past to make artillery. One of the artillery pieces was a giant howitzer, developed by the German army. Called Big Bertha, it could fire a shell weighing over 200 pounds. These shells were fired high into the air from many miles away; when the shells hit a concrete fort, they could destroy it. Artillery fired a variety of shells. Some exploded on impact with a target. Others had fuses that enabled them to explode in the air over the target, dropping metal on the defenders and killing or wounding many of them. Still others had a delayed reaction and did not explode until after they had landed.

WORLD WAR I

Powerful artillery, along with machine guns and automatic rifles, were used by the large armies that met on the battlefields of Europe during World War I. The war lasted four years, from 1914 to 1918. The Central powers—Germany and Austria–Hungary—were pitted against the Allies—France, England, Italy, Russia, and later the United States. Smokeless gunpowder, combined with high explosive substances such as TNT, killed and wounded men by the thousands.

When the war began, most of the battlefield commanders believed that it would be a short conflict. They were accustomed to fighting short wars in Africa against enemies who did not possess powerful weapons. During World War I, however, both sides had equally destructive weapons that could be used to batter each other and create a stalemate. It seems that only the British secretary for war, Lord Herbert Kitchener, recognized what lay ahead. Kitchener warned, "We must be prepared to put armies of millions of men in the field and maintain them for several years."[67]

On the Western Front, German soldiers on one side, and French and British troops on the other side, tried to protect themselves by building miles and miles of trenches guarded by barbed-wire fences. Over the next four years, they battled each other for control of these trench lines. The slaughter that resulted was unlike anything that had ever been seen in history. At the beginning of a battle, an attacking army would fire thousands and thousands of rounds of artillery to try to destroy as many of the enemy as possible. They would then launch an attack, but hundreds would often be mowed down by machine gun fire before they could reach the trenches of the enemy. The entrenched troops often used small trench mortars—artillery pieces that fired arching shells out of a trench toward an

Developed by the German army, Big Bertha was a giant howitzer that could fire shells weighing more than 200 pounds. These shells could destroy concrete walls. The Big Bertha in this photograph was captured by Allied forces during World War I.

attacking enemy. Between 1914 and 1918, all the battles resulted in only a small amount of territory, approximately 10 miles, changing hands between the Allies and the Germans.

In 1916, for example, the French and Germans fought over the fortress of Verdun in France. Before the battle ended in a French victory, 400,000 troops had been killed and 800,000 wounded. A year later at the battle of Passchendaele, the British and French lost another 400,000 men and the German losses were 270,000. During World War I, machine guns using smokeless powder were harnessed to new types of weapons.

These included airplanes that fought each other over the skies of Europe and fired at enemy trench positions on the ground. In addition, planes and huge lighter-than-air balloons called Zeppelins bombed cities and other locations. In 1916, tanks using machine guns and artillery were first introduced in combat. By the following year, they were being used successfully to support infantry attacks and break down barbed-wire defenses in front of the trenches.

For four years, the combatants were locked in a struggle that seemed to have no end. The killing of World War I stopped only after the United States Army entered the war in 1917. These additional troops finally gave the British and French the advantage they needed to defeat the Germans. By the time the war had ended, approximately 10 million people had been killed and 80 million wounded. Many were innocent civilians whose cities had been bombed, and whose countries had been overrun during the war. World War I began the era of total war. New weapons, such as the airplane, could bomb any location and destroy any city. No one was safe.

WORLD WAR II

Following two decades of peace, war broke out again in 1939. By the beginning of World War II, weapons such as the tank and the airplane had become even more effective. Nazi armies commanded by German dictator Adolf Hitler invaded Poland and conquered the country within a few weeks. The Germans used a combination of infantry, tanks, and artillery in one army. A year later, Germany had successfully conquered France and had taken control of most of Western Europe. Only Great Britain remained unconquered. What followed was the German bombing of English cities in an attempt to convince England to surrender. The airplane, using highly explosive bombs, had now become a major weapon in warfare.

In the Pacific, Japan used the airplane to successfully attack the United States at Pearl Harbor, Hawaii, on December 7, 1941.

Many U.S. ships were destroyed. However, the American aircraft carriers were not at Pearl Harbor when the attack occurred. These new ships carried airplanes that could be launched against an enemy. Indeed, the Japanese had used carriers in the attack on Pearl Harbor. Following this attack, Japanese troops overran much of Southeast Asia. Approximately six months after the attack on Pearl Harbor, however, the American carriers launched strikes against the Japanese fleet at the Battle of Midway in the central Pacific Ocean. As a result, the Japanese lost several of their carriers. This was the turning point of the war in the Pacific, and the Japanese went on the defensive.

Meanwhile, in Europe, the Allies slowly began to push back the Nazi armies. The British air force beat back the Nazi planes that were bombing England. Meanwhile the Nazis had invaded the Soviet Union. In 1942, Soviet armies launched a counterattack involving one million soldiers against the German forces. In January 1943, the Germans surrendered at Stalingrad, the turning point of the war on the eastern front. The following year, Allied forces invaded Europe. On June 6, they launched the largest amphibious invasion in world history when more than 175,000 troops came onto the beaches at Normandy in France. By this time the Allies were driving the weaker German air force almost completely out of the skies. With the help of superior air power, the Allies were successful in pushing the Nazis back across Europe until they finally surrendered in April 1945.

In the Pacific, American troops also drove the Japanese back toward their homeland on the islands of Japan. However, it would take the introduction of a new weapon to bring the war to a close. This was not a weapon that used gunpowder, but a new technology. The atomic bomb derived its destructive powers from the splitting of atoms. On August 6, 1945, American planes flew over the city of Hiroshima and dropped the first atomic bomb. It killed 90,000 people. Another atomic bomb was dropped on the city of Nagasaki a few days later. On September 2, 1945, the Japanese surrendered.

On June 6, 1944, approximately 175,000 American troops landed on the beaches of Normandy, France. The soldiers in this photograph have just disembarked from a U.S. Coast Guard landing boat. German troops armed with machine guns wait on the beach.

MODERN WARFARE

Today, smokeless gunpowder continues to be used as a propellant in handheld weapons, like rifles and machine guns, as well as in artillery. During the last half of the twentieth century, these weapons have been fired by thousands of soldiers on battlefields in Korea, Vietnam, the Middle East, and Central Europe. Modern armies also rely on sophisticated technology to guide ground missiles and direct pinpoint bombing attacks from the air against enemy targets. Behind these conventional wars lies the constant threat of nuclear warfare. From the invention of gunpowder during the Middle Ages to the current era, warfare has undergone enormous changes.

A column of smoke topped with a mushroom-shaped cloud hovers over the Japanese city of Nagasaki, where an atomic bomb, dropped by American planes on August 6, 1945, killed 90,000 people. Japan surrendered less than a month later, on September 2, 1945.

Before the invention of gunpowder, wars were fought with spears, swords, and bows and arrows. Today, however, wars are waged on a much grander scale: soldiers now fight with weapons that can kill millions of people instantly. These new advancements raise numerous ethical, economic, and environmental questions about the methods of warfare. While the twenty-first century wrestles with these concerns, the transforming power of gunpowder has become increasingly clear. For better or worse, the invention of gunpowder has revolutionized warfare, and thus the world.

1066	Battle of Hastings; conquest of England by Normans
1099	Jerusalem captured by the Crusaders
1260s	English scientist Roger Bacon experiments with gunpowder
1340	Naval battle of Sluys between France and Britain
1346	English victory over the French at Crecy; first use of cannon in Europe
1400s	Matchlock gun invented in Germany
1415	Battle of Agincourt; victory of Henry V of England over the French
1440s	Charles VII of France wins Hundred Years' War with cannon
1453	Turks capture Constantinople with cannon
1500s	Wheel lock gun replaces matchlock
1521	Cortés captures Aztec capitol of Tenochtitlán with artillery
1532	Pizarro captures king of Incas using early form of musket
1571	Christians defeat Turks with sailing ships and cannon
1600s	Flintlock gun replaces the matchlock
1755	English general Edward Braddock defeated in Ohio by Indians and French using muskets
1775	American Revolution breaks out at Lexington and Concord over gunpowder
1777	American riflemen help defeat British at Battle of Saratoga, turning point of American Revolution
1780–81	American riflemen instrumental in winning war in the South during the American Revolution
1805	Napoleon wins battle of Austerlitz
1807	Reverend Alexander Forsyth patents percussion system
1812	War of 1812 begins between United States and Great Britain
1814	British use rockets fired by gunpowder at attack on Fort McHenry; Francis Scott Key, watching battle, writes *Star-Spangled Banner*
1835	Samuel Colt invents working revolver
1840s	Prussians develop breechloading, needle gun
1849	Minie ball developed
1850s	Rifled muskets become widely used

1857	Lammot DuPont invents "B" powder for mining
1860s	Richard Gatling invents the Gatling gun
1866	Alfred Nobel develops dynamite
1885	French physicist Paul Vieille invents smokeless gunpowder
1880s	Hiram Maxim develops the machine gun
1905	TNT explosive developed
1914–18	Smokeless gunpowder used in artillery, airplanes, tanks, hand grenades, machine guns, pistols and repeating rifles during World War I
1939–45	Smokeless gunpowder used in weapons during World War II
1945	Atomic bombs dropped on Japan

NOTES

Chapter 1: War Begins over Gunpowder

1. Christopher Ward, *The War of The Revolution.* New York: Macmillan, 1952, p.30.
2. William H. Hallahan, *The Day The American Revolution Began.* New York: William Morrow, 2000, p. 23.
3. Ward, *The War of The Revolution,* p. 37.
4. Ibid., p. 30.
5. Ibid., p. 41.
6. Ibid., p. 39
7. Christopher Hibbert, *Redcoats and Rebels: The American Revolution Through British Eyes.* New York: W.W. Norton, 1990, p. 34.

Chapter 2: Early Methods of Warfare

8. John Keegan, *The Book of War.* New York: Viking, 1999, pp. 35-36.
9. Terrence Wise, *Medieval Warfare.* New York: Hastings House, 1976, p. 164.
10. Keegan, *The Book of War*, p. 44.
11. Ibid., p. 45.
12. J.R. Partington, *The History of Greek Fire and Gunpowder*. Camabridge, England: W. Heffer& Sons, LTD., 1960, p. 22.
13. Geoffrey Parker, ed., *The Cambridge Illustrated History of Warfare: The Triumph of the West*. Cambridge, England: Cambridge University Press, 1995, pp. 100-101.
14. Keegan, *The Book of War*, p. 55.
15. Wise, *Medieval Warfare*, p. 119.

Chapter 3: Gunpowder Arrives in Europe

16. Jixing Pan, "The Origin of Rockets in China," in *Gunpowder: The History of an International Technology.* Edited by Brenda Buchanan. Bath, England: Bath University Press, 1996, p. 25.
17. Kelly DeVries, "Gunpowder and Early Gunpower Weapons," in *Gunpowder: The History of an International Technology*, p. 124.
18. Robert Howard, "The Evolution of the Process of Powder Making from an American Perspective," in *Gunpowder*, p. 14.
19. Bert Hall, "The Corning of Gunpowder and The Developement of Firearms in the Renaissance," in *Gunpowder*, p. 89.

20. Parker, *The Cambridge Illustrated History of Warfare: The Triumph of the West*, p. 109.
21. Wise, *Medieval Warfare*, pp. 98-100.
22. W.W. Greener, *The Gun and Its Developement*. New York: Bonanza Books, 1910, p. 47.
23. Wise, *Medieval Warfare*, p. 103.
24. Parker, *The Cambridge Illustrated History of Warfare: The Triumph of the West*, pp. 107-8.
25. Ibid., pp. 113-4.
26. Lord Kinross, *The Ottoman Centuries: The Rise and Fall of the Turkish Empire*. New York: Morrow, 1977, p. 88.
27. Ibid., p. 99.
28. Ibid., pp. 99–100.
29. Thomas Arnold, "War In Sixteenth Century Europe: Revolution and Renaissance" in *European Warfare, 1453-1815*. Edited by Jeremy Black. New York: St. Martin's Press, 1999, p. 38.
30. Ibid., pp. 33-34.
31. Parker, *The Cambridge Illustrated History of Warfare: The Triumph of the West*, p. 125.

Chapter 4: The Conquest of Empires

32. John Dos Passos, *The Portugal Story: Three Centuries of Exploration and Discovery*. Garden City, N.Y.: Doubleday, 1969, p. 171.
33. Ibid., 181.
34. Ibid., p. 204.
35. Ibid., p. 241.
36. Parker, *The Cambridge Illustrated History of Warfare*. p. 133.
37. Hugh Thomas, *Conquest: Montezuma, Cortes, and the Fall of Old Mexico*. New York: Simon Schuster, 1993, p. 158.
38. Ibid., pp. 167-8.
39. Ibid., p. 186.
40. Ibid., 278.
41. Ibid., p.496.
42. Robert Leckie, *A Few Acres of Snow: The Saga of the French and Indian Wars*. New York: John Wiley, 1999, p. 75.
43. Parker, *The Cambridge Illustrated History of Warfare: The Triumph of the West*, p. 127.
44. John Childs, *Warfare in the Seventeenth Century*. London: Cassell and Co., 2001), p. 153.

Chapter 5: The First Rifles and Muskets

45. Parker, *The Cambridge Illustrated History of Warfare: The Triumph of the West*, p. 164.
46. Edward Creasy, *Fifteen Decisive Battles of the World*, http://www.standin.se/fifteen11a.htm.
47. Ibid., p. 13.
48. Jeremy Black, *Warfare in the Eighteenth Century*. London: Cassell, 1999, p. 168.
49. Ibid., p. 168.
50. Ibid., p. 162.
51. Allan Millet and Peter Maslowski, *For the Common Defense: A Military History of the United States of America*. New York: The Free Press, 1984, p. 11.
52. Ibid.
53. Brian Connell, *The Savage Years*. New York: Harper Brothers, 1959, p. 30.
54. Ibid., pp. 54-55.
55. Millet and Maslowski, *For the Common Defense: A Military History of the United States of America*, p. 57.
56. Christopher Ward, *The War of Revolution*. New York: Macmillan, 1952, pp. 106-7.
57. Black, *Warfare in the Eighteenth Century*, p. 118.

Chapter 6: The Weapons Revolution

58. David Gates, *Warfare in the Nineteenth Century*. Hampshire, England: Palgrave, 2001, p. 55.
59. Geoffrey Perret, *A Country Made by War*. New York: Random House, 1989, p. 192.
60. Harold L. Peterson, *Encyclopedia of Firearms*. New York: E.P. Dutton, 1964, p. 120.
61. Ibid., p. 309.
62. Millet and Maslowski, *For the Common Defense: A Military History of the United States of America*, p. 189.
63. Wendy Mitman Clarke, "Pieces of History," *Smithsonian*, November, 2002, p. 66.
64. Millet and Maslowski, *For the Common Defense: A Military History of the United States of America*, p. 229.

Chapter 7: Beyond Gunpowder

65. Perret, *A Country Made by War*, p. 306.
66. Ibid., p. 286.
67. Jeremy Black, ed., *European Warfare, 1815-2000*. Hampshire, England: Palgrave, 2002, p. 80.

BIBLIOGRAPHY

Black, Jeremy. *Warfare in the Eighteenth Century.* London: Cassell, 1999.

Gates, David. *Warfare in the Nineteenth Century.* Hampshire, England: Palgrave, 2001.

Hallahan, William. *The Day The American Revolution Began.* New York: William Morrow, 2000.

Keegan, John. *The Book of War.* New York: Viking, 1999.

Leckie, Robert. *A Few Acres of Snow: The Saga of the French and Indian Wars.* New York: John Wiley, 1990.

Millet, Allan R. and Peter Maslowski. *For the Common Defense: A Military History of the United States.* New York: Free Press, 1984.

Parker, Geoffrey, ed. *The Cambridge Illustrated History of Warfare: The Triumph of the West.* Cambridge, England: Cambridge University Press, 1995.

Perret, Geoffrey. *A Country Made by War.* New York: Random House, 1989.

Thomas, Hugh. *Conquest: Montezuma, Cortes, and the Fall of Old Mexico.* New York: Simon and Schuster, 1993.

Bilby, Joseph G. *Civil War Firearms.* Conshohocken, Pa.: Combined Books, 1996.

Black, Jeremy. *European Warfare, 1453–1815.* New York: St. Martin's Press, 1999.

Chidsey, Donald Barr. *Goodbye to Gunpowder.* New York: Crown Publishers, 1963.

Childs, John. *Warfare in the Seventeenth Century.* London: Cassell, 2001.

Greener, W.W. *The Gun and its Development.* New York: Bonanza Books, 1910.

Kinross, Lord. *The Ottoman Centuries: The Rise and Fall of the Turkish Empire.* New York: William Morrow, 1977.

Millett, Allan R., and Peter Maslowski. *For The Common Defense: A Military History of the United States of America.* New York: The Free Press, 1984.

Parker, Geoffrey, ed. *The Cambridge Illustrated History of Warfare: The Triumph of the West.* Cambridge, England: Cambridge University Press, 1995.

Wise, Terrence. *Medieval Warfare.* New York: Hastings House, 1976.

WEBSITES:

Brief History of Gunpowder
   http://www.argonet.co.uk/users/cjhicks/gphis.html

DuPont Heritage
   http://heritage.dupont.com

The First World War
   http://www.firstworldwar.com

Gunpowder Weapons of the Late Fifteenth Century
   http://xenophongroup.com/montjoie/gp_wpns.htm

Howstuffworks.com: How Flintlock Guns Work
   http://www.howstuffworks.com/flintlock1.htm

NapoleonSeries.com
   http://www.napoleonseries.org

Origins: Life & Death: The Story of Gunpowder
   http://www.sciencenet.org.uk/Origins/gunpowder.html

Sharpshooter: A History of Gunpowder
   http://www.sportshooter.com/reloading/historygunpowder.htm

page:
10: OWI/ National Archives
13: © Bettmann/CORBIS
14: © Bettmann/CORBIS
17: British Library Images
18: ©Robert Estall /CORBIS
21: © Bettmann/CORBIS
25: © Archive Iconografico, S.A. /CORBIS
31: © Hulton Archive, by Getty Images, Inc.
35: © Bettmann/CORBIS
42: © Archive Iconografico, S.A. /CORBIS
45: © Bettmann/CORBIS
49: © Bettmann/CORBIS
54: © Bettmann/CORBIS
59: © Michael Freeman /CORBIS

64: © CORBIS
68: © Francis G. Mayer/CORBIS
71: National Archives
75: © Stapleton Collection/CORBIS
77: © Bettmann/CORBIS
85: National Archives
86: © Bettmann/CORBIS
89: M.F. Steele Collection at US Army
    Military History Institute
91: National Archives
94: © Bettmann/CORBIS
97: National Archives
98: National Archives

Cover: © Michael Freeman/CORBIS
Frontis: © Bettmann/CORBIS

Richard Worth has over 30 years experience as a writer, trainer, and video producer. He has written more than 25 books, including *The Four Levers of Corporate Change*, a best-selling business book. Many of his books are for young adults on topics that include family living, foreign affairs, biography, history, and the criminal justice system.